SWITCHED ON
The Heart and Mind of a Special Agent

ERIC J. CARON

Developmental Editor: Vivien Cooper

First published by Dog Ear Publishing
4011 Vincennes Road
Indianapolis, IN 46268
www.dogearpublishing.net

ISBN: 978-1-4575-6243-3

This book is printed on acid free paper.
Printed in the United States of America

Dedication

To my father, Sgt. Edmond Caron, Jr.,
a man who had so little but gave so much.
To my twin brother, Eddie J. Caron, my soulmate
who taught me the real meaning of life...love!
And to the men and women of law enforcement who sacrifice and serve.
Without these good shepherds, our neighborhoods, cities, states
and country would almost certainly fail to exist.
As it is written in the Holy Bible at John 10:11:
"I am the good shepherd.
The good shepherd sacrifices his life for the sheep."

Foreword

Those who are switched on have a high-functioning internal compass and GPS system. They have emotional equilibrium and dexterity. They recognize nuances in their complex environments, and are guided as to when to turn just a few degrees to the left or right, go forward full throttle, back up, or come to a dead stop.

Being switched on is a daily decision, a moment by moment choice, a constant awareness and mindset. It is a coat of armor that protects you from all types of threats, in all aspects of life. Unless being switched on becomes a part of your very DNA, life itself will be very hard to pull off. Never mind needing to be switched on in a career in law enforcement or government agency work—just walking through our complex and difficult world is hard to safely and effectively navigate these days.

We need to be able to read the people in front of us, behind us, on the phone and online. Being switched on could mean the difference between having your bank accounts hacked or not, and having your identity stolen or not. There could even be a time when being switched on could save your very life. We've all seen news reports of people innocently going to a concert or theater only to be ambushed and gunned down by some maniac with an AK-47. So, we must be in the habit of being switched on.

Education alone is not enough. Training is not enough. Experience is not enough. Someone could have all the book knowledge, all the theoretical knowledge, all the experience in the world and still come up short. Being switched on is the key differentiator. It must become a habit, second nature, part of the very fiber of your being.

I'll never forget an occasion when I was a U.S. Customs Agent and I was sitting in a car in the Bronx, by myself at night. There were several of us agents positioned around the Bronx but I was in my car alone.

Now, the Bronx is a dangerous environment and street crime was all around me. In this particular incident, a load of drugs was sitting in a container in a warehouse and I and my fellow agents were getting ready to pounce. We had a trip wire on the container doors. When the signal was given—the tripping of the wire—we would rush inside and make the arrest.

It was about five o'clock in the morning and I had been up for at least twenty-four hours by this point in time, waiting for the bad guys to show up. They weren't exactly going to send us an email or a text letting us know when they were planning to arrive, so we had no choice but to sit and wait. I had to be constantly switched on, minute by minute, hour by hour, for as long as it took.

There was no room for error. If I had fallen asleep or simply checked out, I could have put myself and fellow agents in grave danger. Because I was alert and aware, the operation went off without a hitch. As soon as the doors were opened and the wire was tripped, we moved in and surprised the importers of the load, successfully arresting and prosecuting them.

Another incident when I was working for U.S. Customs comes to mind. I and my fellow agents were surveilling a container that was in the port of Newark, New Jersey. It was midnight, and our squad needed a couple of agents to be "the eyes in the sky" for the operation. So, a fellow agent and I began to climb up an eight-story warehouse, using the metal pipe ladder on the exterior of the warehouse.

At last, we made it to the roof of the warehouse—the metal roof. Suddenly it started to drizzle. Then the drizzle turned to rain. Then the lightning came. There we were on a metal roof in the rain and lightning. Everyone knows better than to mix water and electricity. So, we began to hustle our way back down off the roof, trying to escape before one or both of us ended up getting electrocuted.

We had been so focused on finding a platform to surveil the bad guys that we could have failed to act in time. Had we kept our attention on our bags of tactical gear, we might not have noticed the lightning off in the distance. Had we not been switched on, and gotten ourselves off that wet, metal roof before lightning struck us, I might not be writing this today.

Sometimes the threat is external, like inclement weather or a bad guy. Sometimes we are required to be switched on in an entirely different way. One incident that is a perfect example of this took place during the time I was an agent with Homeland Security, working out of the U.S. Consulate in Dubai.

People would walk in off the street and say, "I am So-'n'-So from X country, and I want to be an agent for the government...a spy." (We called these people "walk-ins.")

If a walk-in said, for example, "I have some information about terrorists in Jordan and I happen to know they are planning an attack," we obviously couldn't take their words at face value. There was a formal vetting process in place to determine whether a person was sincere in their desire to become an agent, or actually a terrorist or double-agent.

On this particular day, we had a walk-in. A man was standing in front of me and I had to determine whether or not what he was telling me was legitimate. He was Middle Eastern and about twenty-five years old. Right from the very moment he walked into the office, after being screened for weapons and put in a secure interrogation room, I had to be switched on. It was the only way I could do an accurate assessment of him. I had to look at him holistically, from top to bottom.

As the man sat there in the chair and answered my questions, I watched his physical demeanor. Was it different before, during or after the questions? Did he posture back or forward? Did his eyes go high to the right or the left? Did he have trouble looking me in the eye? Did he start sweating when I questioned him? All of those indicators were signs of deception.

What about his words? How did he speak, and how clear and concise was the information he was sharing? If he was vague, it might mean he was a double-agent or a terrorist.

In the case of this particular walk-in, after an in-depth and detailed assessment, I concluded that he was not being truthful. Now, I had to finesse the rejection. If he was indeed a double-agent or terrorist, I could not afford to anger him. And it was not in the agency's best interests to tip him off to the fact that we were onto him.

"Thank you for coming in," I said, attempting to appear neutral. "We will be in touch."

It was a "Don't call us, we'll call you" situation, but I downplayed that and tried to leave him guessing.

Once I had retired from my life as a Special Agent, I couldn't afford to become switched off. Life is always in session, so I have to always be switched on. After all, the world is still the world. I still need to preserve my own life and well-being, and look after and protect my loved ones. And, who knows when I might be in the right place at the right time (or the wrong place at the wrong time, depending on how you look at it) and be called upon to protect perfect strangers.

For example, one night around six o'clock, Marie and I were in Wilmington, North Carolina watching a street guitar player. A small crowd had gathered around to watch him. As I was scanning the crowd, as I always do, one guy in particular caught my eye. He was alone and looked to be a vagrant of some kind. I made a mental note of him.

Fifteen minutes later, Marie and I left the crowd and began to make our way up the street. We got about a block away when that individual I had seen walked up on Marie and me from behind.

He wedged himself between Marie and me and then turned to her with the devil in his eyes. "I'm going to f**k you!" he said.

Then he swiftly walked off ahead of us.

"Cross the street quickly," I said to Marie. "Wait for me over there."

I started walking toward the guy. He saw me, stopped and started walking toward me, as well.

"Get back!" I said loudly and punched him in the chest.

The one-two punch of actually hitting him in the chest and using a loud voice to let him know I meant business did the trick. He backed up until he was standing about ten feet away.

He made a gun sign with his thumb and forefinger, as if to say, "I'm going to shoot you!"

"If he steps back toward me," I instructed a male passerby, "call the police because he's going down!"

The situation did not escalate. The check to the body worked and my words worked. The guy ran away.

I don't have eyes in the back of my head and could not have seen the guy coming. So, he was able to ambush us using the element of surprise. Thankfully, though, I had already scanned the crowd and made a mental note of him. He was already logged in my mental database as an off-kilter, suspicious-looking character.

I had already *read* him. So, as soon as he became a threat—boom! I was able to take quick action. I let him know I was not messing around.

I sent the message to his deranged mind that he needed to stay away from me or I was going to take him down. He was bigger than me but that didn't matter. I let him know who was boss and he got the message loud and clear.

Some might hear this story and say, "But, Eric! With your experience and training, why didn't you just take the guy down? You could have done it easily!"

It was not my goal to fight the guy. I was not interested in ending up on the other end of a knife or a gun. I didn't want to risk contact with his blood, which could have been tainted with HIV or AIDS. And I didn't want to risk contracting any diseases he might have picked up while living on the street.

Now, the thing is, my gun was strapped to my ankle that night. If I had not been switched on, I might have panicked and shot the guy. That's what can happen when a Law Enforcement Officer is not switched on. They get taken by surprise by a bad guy, and react with their trigger finger.

Sure, if I had shot the guy, I may have escaped legal prosecution because it would have been seen as self-defense. But that would have been cold comfort if a man had lost his life because I panicked and shot him. I would have had to live with that for the rest of my life.

And, here is an uplifting story about the potentially life-saving power of being switched on at the right place and right time.

One day while finishing work on this book, my Developmental Editor, Vivien, was out for a walk at a lake located in a large park. She happened to be walking the perimeter of the lake as it neared dusk. Thanks to the lessons she learned while working on this book, she stopped at the beginning of the walking path and reminded herself to be switched on.

As Vivien enjoyed the blue sky, the cool breeze coming off the lake, the dogs out for walks with their owners, and the ducks on the grass, she also had one eye on all the characters she passed on her walk.

Right away at the beginning of her walk, she saw a potentially suspicious character by a tree. She let him know that she saw him by engaging him in direct eye contact, and he backed away. She also noticed a short Hispanic man in a bright white T-shirt. For some reason, her intuition told her to make a mental note of him, despite the fact that he looked like a good man and there was nothing suspicious about him.

Vivien continued on her walk. When she had walked nearly the entire circumference of the lake and was close to the parking lot where she had left her car, a little girl came speeding past her on a scooter.

The girl said nothing and was not crying for help—but because Vivien was switched on, she noticed the girl's distraught expression.

She stopped the girl and asked her what was wrong.

In broken English (Spanish was obviously her first language), the little girl told Vivien that she had gotten separated from her father and little brother. Then she started to cry. This child was riding around on her scooter, trying to bravely find her father—all by herself, as the afternoon sky turned dark, at an enormous lake where she could have easily fallen into the hands of a predator. It was a recipe for disaster.

Thankfully, my editor was at the right place at the right time, and switched on. She was able to stay with the girl and comfort her, while working with a Spanish-speaking Parks & Recreation worker to help reunite this girl with her father and brother.

As Vivien walked the child up to the man that park authorities had identified as the girl's rightful father, she smiled. She realized that it was the same short Hispanic man in the bright white T-shirt that her intuition had told her to remember as she started on her walk.

"I've never seen a man look so relieved," said Vivien. "I had the best feeling as I walked to my car, knowing that because I was switched on, that little girl went home with her family that night, safe and sound."

Sometimes being switched on simply means knowing when to switch *off* and tune out extraneous stimuli. I learned this lesson thanks to the constant pestering I had to endure from agents in another government agency. We called them station agents. They were all about policy making and I was all about catching criminals. So, their end-game goals and mine were almost always at odds.

In every operation, there were a lot of moving parts. And there were times when it would have impeded my efforts to give the station agents what they were asking from me. It didn't always make sense to do a complete information share.

I had to constantly ask myself, *If I stop and give this agent what he's bugging me for, will it slow me down? Will it keep me from doing my best work? And what if I don't give it to him, what's the worst that could happen?*

Sometimes it is better to ask forgiveness than permission.

Then there were those times when it was my integrity that was being threatened. At those times, the threat was much more insidious and snuck up on me. It came to me as a little voice whispering in my ear, a tiny devil on my shoulder.

If I was not in the habit of being switched on at all times, I could have ended up listening to that voice when it was baiting me with messages like, "Take some of the confiscated money and shove it in your pants, Eric. No one will ever know." Or, "Grab some of that cocaine and slip it in the inside pocket of your jacket. You could sell it and no one would ever know."

Agents and police officers go bad all the time, stealing money and drugs because they are not switched on. If I hadn't been switched on at all times during my agency career, I could have wound up in prison, like others I've known in law enforcement and agency work.

Equally importantly, I could have crossed lines, morally, ethically and legally that would have left me with deep shame and a splintered moral foundation. Thanks to being switched on, I was always attuned to threats to my integrity, and always had one eye on my moral compass.

One of the most extreme examples of this type of moral test came while I was assisting on a drug case in beautiful Newark, New Jersey. We had just completed a search and I was asked to transport back to the office half a million dollars in cash. This was an out-of-the-blue request, so I had no time to mentally or spiritually prepare for this task.

I suddenly found myself alone in my car with boxes of money which had not yet been counted. It would have been the easiest thing in the world for me to snatch a few thousand dollars of the money and stuff it down my pants. No one would have ever been the wiser. The thing is, once you've crossed *one* moral line and listened to the devil on your shoulder, it becomes easier and easier to cross bigger and bigger lines.

We see this all the time with drug abusers. Someone tells themselves that they will smoke pot but they'll never use cocaine. Then, they're out at a nightclub one night and someone puts a small silver spoon in front of their nose while they're dancing, and they take a snort, moving the moral line. With some people, this can go on and on until they find themselves scratching their head and wondering how they ended up on Skid Row with a crack pipe in their mouth.

Your only hope is to stop the dominoes before they start falling. You can do this by remaining switched on. That way, you can hear the angel on your other shoulder when it whispers to you, "Don't do it!"

I have such peace in knowing that in my long agency career, I never crossed moral lines that would have made my Police Officer father ashamed of me. After all, he was the one who first taught me the importance of being switched on.

From as far back as I can remember, Dad instilled in my brother and sisters and me the importance of being ready to fight the demons of the world, both internally and externally. He often reminded us that we would be tested. And as you are about to read in these pages, Dad taught us that the way to prepare for those tests was by practicing good self-care, keeping God by our side and putting family first. Dad planted those seeds, and they took root inside me as a boy and began to grow.

Dad trained me to be a mini Marine. So, when I grew up and became a Special Agent for the U.S. Government, I already had that internal foundation. Only, now I had to take that early training to the next level. Now, the stakes were much higher. Everything was riding on my ability to use the tools my father gave me, and all the new ones I learned in school and acquired during Special Agent training.

Thanks to my father, I was one of the lucky ones. I already understood that no amount of classroom or book learning, or even on-the-street experience was going to get anyone very far unless they were in the habit of being switched on. No college degree or training certificate would be enough to keep me safe, or ensure my effectiveness and success on the job and in life.

So, buckle up as I introduce you to my wonderful family and take you on the ride of your life—or the ride of my life, anyway. Along the way, I will take the "secret" out of "secret agent" and give you a glimpse into the heart and mind of this Special Agent.

Acknowledgments

To Eddie, my first love...We were bonded together in utero and in life. You taught me how to love unconditionally. And by living your life the way you did, you showed me that laughter and making others happy are the keys to a happy life. Thank you!

To Dad, my hero...Your core beliefs in family, God and country inspired me. By teaching and training me to practice SEE daily and always remain switched on, you gave me a guiding principle for a lifetime of good self-care. And your acts of love and kindness shaped my heart and mind and helped me grow into the man I have become.

To Mom...Thank you for bringing me into this world and for the love, wisdom and encouragement you imparted to me before departing.

To my five sisters, Deb, Sue, Lynn, Cheryl and Michelle, the girls who taught me how to sing, dance and twirl a baton...You have all taught me well and I am truly grateful.

To my brothers-in-laws, Bruce, Glenn, Randy and John...Thank you for taking such good care of my sisters and being brave enough to walk up the steps of Emery Street for the hours of interrogation by Sgt. Caron.

To Uncle Pete and Aunt Barbara...Thank you for your love and support. You both left this world too early.

To Uncle Bob and Uncle Jack... Thank you for stepping in when my father died. I so appreciate you giving of yourselves, and loving and supporting not only me but the entire Caron clan. I know that there have been times when you have sacrificed your own family time in the process, and it has not gone unnoticed or unappreciated.

To my sons, Jacob and Tyler, my gifts from God...You both appeared in my life at the opportune time, just as God planned. You opened up the beautiful world of fatherhood to me and your wholehearted trust in me, and dependence upon me, made me a better man. I look forward to being right by your side as you journey on through life. I am so proud of you!

To Marie…Thank you for encouraging me to write my story. Our thirty years together was adventurous and exciting, as we traveled the world together and grew. As my wife and partner, you endured many sleepless nights worrying, and constant family meals and events interrupted by my Bat phone. Thank you for your love and patience during those years.

To Aunt Carol…You have opened your heart and home to me and my family. I am forever grateful.

To all my friends, past and present…Your presence in my life has meant more to me than I could express.

To Fr. Tom McElroy and Fr. Richard Gendreau…Thank you for being spiritual compasses for me, helping me find faith during dark days.

To Sensei John Marando…Thank you for helping me take my practice of self-discipline, self-confidence and self-defense to the next level. You're a gift to me and to the community.

To my teachers and professors at Greater New Bedford Regional Voc-Tech High School and Northeastern University…I am forever grateful to you for inspiring my love of learning and guiding me on a path to success.

And last but not least, to my friend and Developmental Editor, Vivien Cooper…Thank you for your patience and for helping me to tell my life story. Your guidance along this journey has been magical. We have laughed and cried together during the birthing of my book. I am so very proud of our creation and thankful to God for putting you in my life.

I love each of you, and the love, kindness and support you have given me will forever be part of who I have become!

✔ Putting Family First and Having a Strong Work Ethic

My father, Edmond J. Caron, was a hard-working Law Enforcement Officer. Dad was born in 1934 in New Bedford, Massachusetts, and grew up in the post-Depression era. He was idolized by me and our entire family.

My father's mother was an uneducated Canadian immigrant who worked as a barmaid in a city bar. Dad's father was a laborer, who dug sewer holes in New Bedford. Grandpa had a heart attack while driving, and died tragically when my dad was only eight years old. His death left my father's immigrant mother and his two younger siblings poverty-stricken.

When he was in the seventh grade, Dad stopped attending school and went to work as a shoeshine boy in New Bedford to help provide for the family. On November 24th, 1954, at nineteen, my father joined the Marine Corps and arrived at Quantico, Virginia. He would later serve in the Korean War and take up playing the trumpet, becoming good enough to join the Marine Corps Band and play throughout the Washington, D.C. area.

After his military service, Dad decided to join the New Bedford Police Department. On August 19th, 1962, he was appointed as a New Bedford Police Officer. He worked as many extra details as he could and when that wasn't quite enough to make ends meet, he took on second and third jobs. He worked as a butcher and as a longshoreman, unloading vessels in the port of New Bedford.

There was also a brief period of time when my parents used food stamps to help feed us. I am sure my dad couldn't have been proud to accept state assistance but with nine mouths to feed, he had little choice. That's right—there were seven of us kids!

Once married, Mom and Dad had four daughters. They loved and adored my sisters but Dad still longed for a son and dreamed that one day, a boy would join the family. On July 24th, 1965, Dad's dream came true when he was surprised with the birth of not one son but two—me and my fraternal twin brother, Eddie. Another daughter was to follow later.

When Eddie and I were toddlers, we were notorious for climbing out of our crib and wreaking havoc. With four other children under the age of ten to look after, my mother couldn't spend all her time chasing after my brother and me. One day, she had an idea. She got an extra set of my Dad's handcuffs and cuffed our tiny legs to the crib.

I still wouldn't stay put. When I was three, I somehow removed the screen on a window and wandered onto the bulkhead that dropped twelve feet down to the ground.

My mother couldn't believe her eyes when she saw me essentially out on the ledge. Thankfully, she was able to coax me back inside by pleading with me.

✔ Building a Strong Foundation of Integrity and Faith

Eddie and I spent a lot of time on Dad's knees watching sports and World War II documentaries. And each evening, Dad would lead us in our prayers.

My father was a man of high integrity, honesty and faith. When it was prayer time, Dad would enter our bedroom, stand by the bunkbed I shared with Eddie and extend one hand to him on the bottom bunk and the other hand to me on the top. Then it was time for prayers.

These prayers centered around thankfulness and forgiveness. Dad would always start by saying: "Heavenly Father, thank you for this day and for keeping me and my family safe from the evils of the world. Thank you, God, for providing me with a beautiful wife and family. Thank you, God, for our military men and women who have served our country. And keep us safe while we sleep."

Dad would also thank God for the simple necessities of life—food, shelter, clothes and the oil that kept us all warm during the winter months. And he asked for strength to be the best dad he could be.

✔ Taking Nothing for Granted

"Tomorrow is promised to no one, boys!" my father would say. "Death is like a thief in the night. You never know when it will appear!"

Death was a constant theme during prayer time. He would name all the souls of the faithfully departed, including his father whom he barely remembered. Then he would recognize those who made the ultimate sacrifice and never returned home. (The Vietnam War was raging during my first ten years of life.) Dad also taught us that we must be good, honest people because we will all be judged by God on the day we die.

Dad always ended prayer time with The Lord's Prayer: "Our Father, who art in Heaven, hallowed be thy name; thy kingdom come, thy will be done on earth as it is in Heaven. Give us this day our daily bread; and forgive us our trespasses as we forgive those who trespass against us; and lead us not into temptation, but deliver us from evil, for thine is the kingdom, and the power, and the glory forever and ever. Amen."

With that he would say goodnight, tell us that he loved us and seal it with a kiss.

✔ Being Prepared for Life's Tests

Dad looked at day-to-day life as a test and instilled in us an appreciation of fitness and preparedness. He said, "You never know when you'll be tested. And there might not be a makeup test because you may be dead!"

He always preached about being mentally and emotionally ready for the tests. He developed our hearts through faith and our minds through education. Although not formally educated, Dad understood the importance of education and always stressed it to us kids. Dad taught us that in order to pass the tests of daily life, you must always be ready to perform, whether at work, at school, in relationships or when looking after your own security.

As a Police Officer, my father witnessed bad guys' actions and saw firsthand what could befall the victims. So, he also wanted us physically strong to fight back the evils of the world. As far as he was concerned, there was no way you could stay mentally strong and prepared unless you were in good physical condition.

Dad developed our bodies through good sleep, diet and exercise. He believed it was essential to get a good night of sleep, follow proper nutrition and exercise daily. He always enjoyed seeing our fridge and cupboards stacked with healthy food. And, although we had very little money, he bought us weights to work out with, and made us a wooden flat bench. Eddie and I played all the usual kid sports too: football, baseball and basketball.

We were expected to be in bed at a reasonable time (eight o'clock during the school week). Before hitting the rack, we did our nightly pushups and sit-ups. My father always stressed the importance of staying in shape. And he taught us that this sleep-eat-exercise routine was the foundation for a healthy, well-balanced life. (I coined this "SEE" so it would be easy to remember.)

The seed of SEE stems from my dad's Marine Corps training. He turned Eddie and me into young Marines. Later in life, I would pass along Dad's SEE philosophy to my own children and any of their friends who would listen. It became so ingrained in my children that I could simply hold up three fingers at the dinner table. My kids would race to see who could say "SEE!" the fastest.

To this day, my children can instantly recite SEE. They understand the need for eight hours of sleep, a balanced diet with limited sugar and fat, and moderate exercise daily, or three or four days a week at the very least. The SEE mantra is simple and maybe that's why I like it. I think this country—and in fact, the entire world—would be much better off if we all practiced SEE in our daily lives.

As I grew up and became a Special Agent, I came to think of being ready for life's tests as being "switched on." Switched on means you are operating with all your senses, staying alert, and running on all cylinders.

✔ Living Together as a Team

Our family lived in a modest cottage with a single bathroom for all nine of us—two adults and seven kids whose ages ranged within one decade of pregnancies and births. With such a large family, teamwork was essential. Without it, our daily lives would have been chaotic.

Interestingly, being raised as a team seemed to immunize us kids against sibling rivalry. I have many wonderful memories related to being part of such a large family, including parties, the constant flow of siblings' friends, boyfriends and girlfriends, and listening to music that spanned several decades.

We also learned that patience was a virtue in the Caron clan. Our patience was tested each and every morning for nearly fifteen years, with just one bathroom that measured five by five and featured one single sink. Getting ready for church on any given Sunday, for example, was quite the production.

The Caron clan bathroom dance went like this: The line would start at six o'clock each and every morning. My dad was usually first into the bathroom to shave so he could make police roll call. Meanwhile Mom was busy in the kitchen preparing breakfast and packing our lunch boxes. Then the line for the bathroom went pretty much in order of age.

Deb entered the bathroom first and brushed her teeth. Sue entered and used the toilet, then Deb entered the shower. Sue then moved over to the sink to brush her teeth. Lynn then entered, and used the toilet as Deb jumped out of the shower. Sue then got into the shower. Deb left the bathroom in a towel and Lynn brushed her teeth while Cheryl used the toilet.

By the time Eddie and I entered into the bathroom dance, most of the hot water was gone. So, to add to the morning excitement, we would intentionally flush the toilet and listen to our sisters scream. That was our only hope of getting them out of the shower so we could have a shot at some warm water. Our youngest sister Michelle, who went in after us, had no chance at all.

This organized chaos went on for more than an hour every single morning, with three to four kids using the toilet, brushing their teeth, shaving, showering and/or blow-drying their hair.

The Caron bathroom dance prepared us for life's challenges. It taught us early in life that patience is necessary to live in harmony, and teamwork is essential to be successful in anything you do. If we were all to make it out the door in time to make it to the school bus stop a few blocks away, we needed patience and the help of each other. My older sisters were always helping Eddie and me get dressed for school and making sure we had our homework completed and in hand. There was certainly no letter "I" in the Caron team.

Every Sunday, we attended church wearing our homemade clothes stitched by my mother and Nana Bolger. Once our bathroom rotations were completed and we were all dressed in our Sunday best, we would pile into the station wagon that my Dad bought for a dollar from a close friend. After mass, we would drive over to visit our maternal grandparents and sometimes our paternal grandparents as well.

As the Caron procession walked into church led by my parents, Dad would stand by a pew and watch us all genuflect and make the sign of the cross. If one of us did it incorrectly or haphazardly, Dad would signal to us to try again. Anyone who might have been sitting in the pew before we all filed in got squeezed out.

Once settled in with our dad on the end, we would all kneel and pray. Eddie and I would pray that we didn't get a backhand in the head for laughing at someone or something. We would often pass gas and then it was all over for us.

1954 - Dad - A young Marine

Dad - Member of the Marine Corps Marching Band

On most Sundays, the last song of the mass was *Let There Be Peace on Earth*. At the time, I was puzzled when I would see my big strong Police Officer father get emotional at the first note of this song. As a child, I didn't really fully understand the meaning of these lyrics: *Let there be peace on earth, and let it begin with me…*

It wasn't until much later in life that I truly understood the message of this song and got emotional myself during mass with my family. I started considering the lyrics in light of all the hurt and crime that happens all around us each day. I also started thinking about how many bad guys threaten the peace of individuals, families, and country.

"Let there be peace on earth, and let it begin with me" is a great approach to life.

✔ Learning to Be Respectful of Others

Grocery shopping for a family of nine was an all-day, two-person team sport, especially as we kids grew older. When I would go along to the grocery store, my mom made sure Eddie stayed home, and vice versa. Otherwise, she would spend most of the time keeping us out of trouble, preventing fights between us or stopping us from making fun of people.

Eddie and I would go to the shelves, take items down and leave them on the ground, and then pass the buck to each other when we got in trouble.

Or, I would see someone who was overweight and say, "Hey, Eddie, look at that fatso! She's had too much pasta or ice cream."

Mom would hear this and say, "Eric! Eddie! That's not very Christian of you! Get back on the carriage and don't get off."

Or, Eddie might start prancing down the aisle, imitating people and acting silly. And then I would join in and we would start walking like ladies. Or, we would role-play over buying something,

"So, Eddie," I would say, "what do you think? You want steak for dinner?"

"No…fish!"

✔ Watching My Mother Put Us First

Whenever we were grocery shopping, Mom would embarrass me by saying, "Eric, this cart's full. Go get another one." On some weeks, we bought so much food, a third cart was required.

As the Caron food train made its way to the checkout counter, customers began to run ahead of us toward the checkout line. Nobody wanted to get stuck behind us in line. I wanted to check out too—out the front door, that is!

I was always mortified by the amount of food we bought and how long it took to check out. (My mortification was made worse by the occasional food stamps and coupons.) I figured that people were looking at our carts, and then looking at us and thinking, "How much food can those people eat?" They didn't see the rest of our huge family, waiting at home.

As the Caron food train rolled out the front door of Fernandes Supermarket, the neighborhood grocery store, we often had to contend with the weather. From December to April, we were met with the harsh New England cold, snow and rain.

In looking back now as an adult, I see what a blessing it was that we could afford enough food to fill the shopping carts, our station wagon and our bellies. And, I think of my frail mother—this five-foot, ninety-eight-pound lady with rheumatoid arthritis throughout her body—and I appreciate what it must have taken for her to do the weekly grocery shopping for her family. Doing this even though she was in tremendous pain was an act of love. It was her way of putting us first.

Loading up the station wagon with dozens of bags of food was a reminder of why no more than one of us kids could go along to the supermarket at a time. There wouldn't have been room in the car for all the food.

Once arriving home, Mom would beep the horn to signal all available hands on deck. Then we actually formed a human train and passed the bags from the car into the kitchen. There was still no time to rest because all the food needed to be put away and, on most days, dinner prepared.

When summertime rolled around, we often made family trips to the beach that was only a quarter mile from our home. These beach outings started with Mom pulling out the bagged loaf of Sunbeam White Bread and making as many peanut-butter-and-jelly or peanut-butter-and-marshmallow-fluff sandwiches as she could before the bread ran out.

Once all the sandwiches had been made and our beachgoing supplies collected, each of us Caron kids would march down the street, responsible for carrying his or her own towels and toys.

My mother would lead the pack and Eddie, Michelle and I would be holding the hands of our older siblings. We would often sing songs such as *The Little Brown Jug, Skip to My Lou* and *The Ants Go Marching.* We were like a modern-day version of the Von Trapp family from *The Sound of Music.*

At the beach, we played for hours, digging and making delicious sand pies. And, we all took swimming lessons throughout the day. By 3:00 p.m., we began the cleanup routine and marched home to get ready for dinner.

✔ Overcoming Obstacles and Dreaming Big

During childhood, I had many painful ear infections requiring tubes in my ears. I still recall being rocked, usually by my dad who was trying to soothe the pain. Ultimately, my ear troubles required several surgeries. Like dominoes falling, my ear problems affected my hearing; my hearing problem affected my speech; and my hearing and speech problems affected my ability to learn.

I was left with slow speech development, hearing loss and a learning disability. I had to repeat second grade and Eddie repeated it with me. It was only much later in life that I learned from my brother and my mother that Eddie had actually passed second grade but my father insisted on keeping us together. I continued to struggle all the way through grammar school and wouldn't truly hit my stride until college.

I recall going to a special-needs clinic to assist in my development. This clinic served all forms of handicapped ("special needs") kids. Although it may have helped me physically, it left emotional scars and affected my self-esteem.

Despite my academic struggles throughout grammar school, I had big dreams and so did my twin brother. He dreamed of becoming a football coach and I dreamed of becoming a Police Officer like our dad.

I would spend my nights listening to the police scanner, and chasing fire trucks and police cars, even during backyard basketball games with Eddie. My obsession was fueled by the proximity of the fire station to our house—it was at the top of our street. I would immediately stop playing with my brother and jump on my bike so I could tail the squad car or fire truck to the call. It drove Eddie nuts when I did that.

When I was ten, I got to accompany my dad on an overnight security detail. From 11:00 p.m. to 8:00 a.m., Dad was assigned to watch over vendors' goods at a summertime festival on the city's waterfront.

My father always worked long hours. When he wasn't working or sleeping, he was volunteering as a baseball coach or providing assistance for the activities my older sisters were involved in, from cheerleading to majorettes.

The thought of staying up all night with my dad was so exciting. Every few hours we would walk the area and then go sit in dad's police car and talk about police work.

"Dad? Can I get on the radio?" I asked.

"Sure," he said. "You can ask for a time check."

So, in the deepest man's voice I could conjure up, I said, "Control, can I have a time check?"

When a voice came back over the radio with the time, it was my thrill for the night. I thought, *Wow! Someone's actually on the other side of this frickin' radio!*

There I was, getting a chance to be at work with my Police Officer father. I spent all night with him, watching him interact with people, protect the public and walk the beat. I tried my best to stay awake all night but by 3:00 a.m., I was fast asleep on my father's lap.

I experienced a kind of doublemindedness that night. On one hand, I was happy and excited to be with my dad and watch him work. On the other hand, I knew that things could potentially change in a New York minute. I was a little afraid but at the same time, I knew my father was right by my side and wearing his gun.

✔ Doing the Right Thing—Not the Easy Thing

As part of instilling in us kids the importance of developing a strong character, Dad taught us to do the right thing—not the easy thing. He stressed honesty and integrity above all else. His mantra was: "Never lie, always tell the truth and do the right thing at all times."

Any time Eddie and I were ever caught lying, we could expect a few kicks in the butt. These lessons about integrity and good character formed the foundation of my life and to this day, they stick with me.

One particular Little League game when I was eleven stands out in my memory. Eddie was the catcher and I pitched most games. We were both good players. Playing Little League Baseball was exciting for us both.

When I got tired out, the coach would come to the mound with Eddie and ask us to switch positions. As Eddie handed me his shin pads, chest protector, helmet and mask, he would reach down into his underwear and pull out his athletic cup. I casually placed it down my pants to the laughter of the fans watching. We were so innocent, we thought nothing of it.

I was having a very frustrating game and struck out at bat. I threw down my baseball bat and helmet. This was a day when my father wasn't coaching. Since I knew he was working, I assumed that he wasn't there watching. With Dad out of sight, I freely vented my frustrations, having no idea that he had jumped the first-base side fence.

I then felt something I was all too familiar with—a size eleven shoe up my ass all the way to the dugout. Every once in a while, I can still feel that size eleven. It's a constant reminder that my father's always watching me. I learned early in life that good character is doing the right thing when no one is watching.

Another Little League game also became a reminder to do the right thing. Eddie and I were playing and Dad was coaching. I was rounding third base and heading into home to score. Instead of sliding, I went into home plate standing. I did this intentionally so I could take out the catcher. I didn't particularly like the guy so I figured I was justified.

In front of packed stands, my dad came out of the dugout and kicked my butt from home plate into the dugout.

I couldn't understand why he was mad. After all, I had scored.

The truth was, my dad recognized that my intention was to hurt the catcher. The end surely didn't justify the means to Coach Caron. This was a life lesson—a lightbulb moment that would stick with me even decades later.

✔ Learning to be Considerate of Others

When Eddie and I were twelve, we were especially rambunctious. During hot and humid New England summer nights, we were always up talking and laughing about the day's events long after midnight when the rest of the Caron clan was trying to sleep.

My father would make several attempts to quiet us down by yelling at us from his bed, but they would inevitably fail. Then, he would march down the hallway like the Marine Sergeant he was, order us up and out of our beds, and march us out the door in our underwear and Kmart sneakers.

"Okay, boys," he would say. "You've got some extra energy, so start running and don't stop until I tell you!"

He was killing two birds with one stone—teaching us a lesson in consideration, and also getting us to burn off some of our excess energy so we and the rest of the household could get some sleep.

Eddie and I headed across the street. We started to run around the entire schoolyard while Dad kept a watchful eye from the front porch and smoked a cigarette.

During one of our midnight runs, we heard another man's voice calling to us in the darkness. "Eddie? Eric? Is that you out there?"

"Yes, Mr. Pomfret," we responded, sheepishly. "It's us."

Evidently, our next-door neighbor couldn't sleep either and was brought outside by the sounds of Eddie and me talking and laughing while we ran.

"What the hell are you doing?" Mr. Pomfret asked. "It's one in the morning!"

"Yes Mr. Pomfret, we know...we're getting some exercise," Eddie said.

Then, just like my father, Mr. Pomfret took a seat on his porch, opened a beer, and watched the show. At some point, he began laughing at us.

That was my brother and me—the after-hours neighborhood entertainment for the night.

After about an hour had passed with Eddie and me running around in the dark, Sgt. Caron would order us back into the house.

"Now, get to bed and don't speak a word or you'll be back outside!"

After those midnight runs, my brother and I slept pretty darned well and never did find ourselves back outside.

✔ Teaching Us the Importance of Discipline

Any of my sisters' boyfriends who entered our house on Emery Street did so at their own risk. Sgt. Caron had the kind of reputation that struck fear into the hearts of young suitors.

Dad would take great pleasure in watching these young men nervously walk up the stairs to the house, through the door, and down the long hallway into the dining room where he held court.

Once my father had the young suitor in front of him, he gave him the short list of do's and don'ts. "Do respect my daughter! And don't even think about returning her home later than 10:00 p.m. And 10:00 means 10:00…not 10:01."

On many nights while my sisters were out on dates with these young men, Eddie and I would spend the evening watching Red Sox games with our dad. As 10:00 approached, Dad would start checking his watch and looking out the windows. He would be muttering under his breath, "They'd better be here by 10…or else!"

Like clockwork, whatever sister was on a date that night would arrive home early with their date, and sit in the car "talking" under the watchful eye of our father.

If my sisters weren't inside the house by 10:00 on the dot, they got the light switch. The front porch light was a beacon and an alarm, signaling them to get their butts inside the house, *now!*

Very rarely did Dad need to hit that light switch twice. On those rare occasions that he did, he would remind my sisters, "10:00 means 10:00!"

Sometimes, if we were lucky, Eddie and I got the privilege of hitting the light switch and creating a light show for our sisters. Then we would watch out the window, laughing, as they hurried inside.

✔ Remaining Heroic to the End

It was July 1st, 1981, a sunny summer day. It was just a few weeks shy of my sixteenth birthday—a birthday I shared not only with my twin brother Eddie but also my older sister Lynn. As I worked washing dishes at a local country club, my cousin Audrey (my mother's sister's daughter) suddenly appeared.

"You need to come home with me, Eric," she said.

While we were walking out of the country club, I turned to Audrey and said, "He died, didn't he? Please tell me!"

With tears streaming down her cheeks, she simply said yes.

Days earlier, Dad had driven himself while on duty to the E.R., and collapsed from a heart attack. He was only forty-six years old. He was my hero, our family's foundation and heart, and a decorated New Bedford, Massachusetts Police Offer.

The entire Caron clan gathered around Dad's hospital bed including my mother, my five sisters (Deb, Susan, Lynn, Cheryl and Michelle), my twin brother Eddie and me. (At the time, our ages ranged from twelve to twenty-two.)

Dad was a Marine to the very end. He demonstrated tremendous courage, expending his precious energy trying to talk to each child individually while connected to a catheter and all sorts of tubes.

This was courage Dad had learned as a young Marine serving in Korea and as a Police Officer. One time while on duty, for example, he had to crawl into a local pharmacy and arrest an armed gunman holding the owner at gunpoint. Later that year, he was awarded Police Officer of The Year for his bravery.

When it was our turn to hear what Dad wanted to say to us, Eddie and I stood on either side of his bed. With the nurses hustling around us, my father whispered to us both, "Take care of your mother and sisters and be good boys."

The day after the family gathered around my father's hospital bed, he was transferred to Mass General Hospital where he died.

✔ Facing the Impossible

As Audrey and I made the twenty-minute drive to the south end of New Bedford, tears poured. I was now fatherless and the security he'd given me was shattered.

I thought, *No Dad to pray with…to watch a Red Sox game with…to play catch with…to watch movies with…to celebrate my sixteenth birthday with in a few weeks.*

As I walked up my front stairs, I realized, *This house is no longer a home.*

The home where we had all experienced so much joy, love and kindness throughout the years was now a house of pain. Death instantly changed all that was good and normal into fear and uncertainty.

Meanwhile, my sisters and mother were traveling back from Mass General Hospital, and Eddie was traveling home from a football camp in the city. (Someone in the family called the coach and he had gotten word to my brother.)

Within the hour, I saw the Mayor's Cadillac speeding up my driveway. Behind the wheel was my dad's brother, Uncle Pete, who was also a New Bedford Police Officer. Inside the car were my five sisters and my mother, who were returning home from Mass General with Uncle Pete.

As I peeked out a parlor window to watch, all the Cadillac doors simultaneously swung open. My mom and sisters got out of the car and were met by other grieving family members. I could hear the sobs, as everyone was forced to face the reality of my dad's death. I had been praying and hoping that Uncle Pete would tell me that Dad was really alive so I could awaken from this nightmare. I now knew that wasn't going to happen.

My entire family and all of our friends began to arrive to pay their respects and help in any way they could. Everyone was sobbing and sharing their grief.

As people were arriving, I witnessed "Uncle" Bob, my dad's very closest friend, in my parents' bedroom. He was in my dad's closet, going through his clothes and laying out my dad's uniform on the bed for the wake.

Seeing Uncle Bob choking back tears drove home the reality that my dad was gone forever. Minutes later as we gathered around the kitchen table, the Chief of Police was heard on the local radio station announcing my father's death. He too could be heard fighting back tears.

✔ Cherishing Special Memories

It was also a day of love and meaningful caring. Many came not to speak but just to be present and listen to stories about Sgt. Caron.

I recounted a memory of my dad being high up a ladder, painting the front of the house. Suddenly, I heard a couple arguing and swearing at each other. They were in the schoolyard across the street, in the middle of some sort of domestic disturbance.

I heard Dad say, "Hey, watch your language there!"

The man looked at my father and said those dreaded two words: "F**k You!"

Dad was the nicest guy but he was known to go high to the right fast over cursing, especially when he heard the F-bomb.

When I heard the guy cursing at my father, I wanted to say, "Oh, that's the wrong thing to say to Sgt. Caron, buddy! I wouldn't say that if I were you!"

I knew what was coming, and I was right. While I watched from the front window, Dad hustled down the ladder, confronted the man, grabbed him by his ponytail and instantly took him to the ground. All I heard was the guy's head hitting the cement in the middle of the street and my dad yelling to my mom, "Hey, Pat! Call the station and have my brother respond!"

Dad needed backup from Uncle Pete and he also needed a cruiser to transport the guy.

From inside the house, I could hear the voice coming over the police scanner: "Unit 23, respond to the Caron house on Emery. Your brother requires assistance."

Within seconds, I heard sirens and the screeching of tires coming around the corner. The cruiser was barely parked before my dad picked up the man and threw him in the back seat, assisted by Uncle Pete, who stood six-foot-four and weighed two-hundred-fifty pounds.

The next thing I heard on the scanner was, "Unit 23 to Control. One in custody heading to St Luke's."

My dad's reaction to the F-bomb had everything to do with his belief that we should all respect and honor ourselves and others. Dad loved, respected and honored his family—and all people. He also loved, respected and honored his country and the flag that represented freedom.

On many Red Sox televised game days, Dad would make Eddie and me stand alongside him in our parlor and salute during the National Anthem. While playing outside in the yard, if our anthem was heard, all playing stopped and we stood at attention or risked getting a size eleven up our butts.

"Remember, freedom isn't free!" Dad would always remind us. "Many soldiers lost their lives for us."

Dad himself was injured while serving in Korea. I have photos of him recovering at a hospital in Japan. He never shared how he got injured but he could often be seen wiping a tear after The National Anthem. He realized how fortunate he was to escape serious injury and death during his military service. He always took a moment to remember and appreciate the sacrifice of those soldiers who didn't make it home.

✔ Honoring Our Fallen Hero

Once everyone had gone home and darkness fell upon us that first night after my dad's passing, all sense of security was lost. My mother went to bed with my dad's photo and she could be heard crying throughout the night.

Eddie and I lay in our bunkbeds adjacent to our parents' bedroom. We listened to our mother sobbing, and talked about how hard it was to believe that Dad was really gone. We cried over how badly we would miss all the things Dad used to do with us—and all the things he would never be able to do with us for the rest of our lives.

Then it hit us that he wouldn't be in to say our prayers with us that night, or any other night. So, we held hands and prayed as our father taught us to do, and added him to the list of all the faithful departed souls.

Around 11:00 that night, we heard yelling outside in the adjacent schoolyard. Fear came over me and no doubt the rest of the family.

Then I remembered my dad's deathbed instructions—to be a good person and take care of my mother and sisters. So, I called the police and within minutes, they arrived and pushed those disturbing the peace out of the schoolyard.

The reality set in as I woke up the same way I went to sleep—hearing the sounds of my mom crying for my dad. Eddie and I endured this nightly and morning torture for many months.

A few days later was the wake, my very first. It was attended by nearly a thousand people and the line snaked around the funeral home parking lot. Now instead of the Caron clan standing around a hospital bed with nurses who were busy trying to keep Dad alive, we were all standing around a coffin with Police Honor Guards.

It was a very long and emotional day. After everyone had left, I decided to stay behind by myself to spend alone time with Dad. Uncle Bob and I shared this moment of grief. He was simply present, saying little. I cried over my father and touched his cool skin for the last time.

My world was truly rocked by the sudden death of my father. I made a promise to him that I would make him proud, follow in his footsteps and live his legacy. I was living for two now.

The funeral was at St. James Church, where on most Sundays the Caron clan took up an entire pew. On the day of the funeral, there were so many cars and buses, the police closed down the streets around the church, filled to capacity. With Eddie on one side of my mom and me on the other, we led the procession behind the casket. I was full of emotions—sadness, nervousness and pride all at the same time.

During the mass, a young priest named Gus Kennedy stood and gave the eulogy. At the end of it, he congratulated my father on a job well done in raising seven children and living a life of love and dedication. Then he brought more than a thousand people to their feet for a standing ovation.

Mayor Jack Markey ("Uncle" Jack) gave a heartfelt remembrance. In it, he described my dad as a man of great character and integrity—a man who believed deeply in God and service to country and family. Then Uncle Jack told a funny story about when Dad was asked to serve as his security detail.

"I want you to know," said my father, "I didn't vote for you. And if you're corrupt, I'll arrest you!"

It was a lighthearted moment and the whole church laughed—but those who knew Officer Caron believed every word.

Prior to saying our final goodbyes at the funeral home, I placed in the casket with Dad a homerun baseball that Eddie had hit. It was cradled between Dad's right forearm and ribs. The ball had been signed by Eddie and me. We simply wrote, "Love You, Dad. We'll Always Be Together."

The *Battle Hymn of the Republic* was the last song played while we all exited the church. As my twin brother and I walked our mother out of the church to the sounds of the music, all we could see everywhere we looked was a sea of blue. Hundreds of Police Officers were lining the church steps and saluting to the hymn.

My mother whispered to Eddie and me, "Sing, boys...sing! Do it for your father."

By encouraging us to sing along, Mom was encouraging everyone to join in, including the men and women in uniform. She knew what a patriotic Marine Dad was, and knew what it would have meant to him.

As we made our way to the cemetery to say our final goodbyes, it was a beautiful New England July day, full of sunshine. We placed a single rose on the casket.

Before returning to the limo, I saluted and walked away. It is a day permanently engraved in my mind.

✔ Finding the Blessings in Tragedy

Dad was on earth one day and gone the next. Despite having so many children, he did not have a life insurance policy. So, in addition to being left fatherless, we were left in difficult financial straits.

I was resentful and angry at God for taking my father when I was only fifteen years old. It didn't seem fair that Dad—a good, honest man who served his country and was faithful to his family—was suddenly taken. Yet, the dregs of society were out walking around, hurting and killing people.

I often thought of Dad's deathbed wish: "Be good boys and take care of your mother and sisters." It would inspire me on most days and haunt me on others.

The weight of living for two was a heavy burden and at times, I struggled with excessive alcohol use and depression. Eddie did too. Thankfully, my basic nature of looking for the silver lining allowed me to survive Dad's passing. Had I been wired differently, I might have fallen into the pit of depression and been unable to climb out.

When I was at my strongest, I was even able to pull the blessings from my dad's death. It was a constant reminder to me of certain things he had taught me. These are some of the lessons that I carry with me in my heart:

- tomorrow is promised to no one
- we must take nothing for granted
- we must be ever vigilant, switched on, and prepared for life's tests
- we must follow our dreams and take those hard steps forward
- if we do, we will be rewarded in life
- we should always honor and respect family, God and country

✔ Fighting the Good Fight

As Eddie and I were struggling to adjust to our dad's death, Mom's health struggles worsened and we were faced with another huge emotional challenge.

Mom had been crippled with arthritis in her hands for many years by that point, and had been battling depression since the death of Dad. Then, in September of 1981, about two months after my dad's death, Mom found a tumor behind her left ear. While the doctor was removing it, he cut a nerve, leaving Mom with facial paralysis and disfigurement.

She was already a tiny, arthritic woman and now her face was also disfigured. I felt so badly for my mom, having that disfigurement, but I also felt embarrassed by her. I was only sixteen years old and at that age when peer acceptance was everything.

When the tumor grew back a year later, Mom's doctor threw up his hands and said, "I'm sorry but I'm afraid there's nothing more I can do."

My mom and my sister Sue had an idea. They thought that maybe Uncle Jack's wife, Aunt Carol, being the wife of the mayor, might have some connections or contacts at a Boston hospital.

So, they paid Aunt Carol a visit. "Surely, there must be *something* we can do!" they said.

Aunt Carol made some calls and arranged for Mom to see a doctor at Mass General.

When Mom got to the hospital, the tumor was removed again. Unfortunately, while Mom was having the tumor removed, the doctors discovered that the cancer had spread to her brain.

Now Mom had to undergo chemotherapy. Being so petite, she was devastated by the treatments. Chemotherapy had a terrible effect on her tongue and prevented her from eating comfortably. During this period, she would cry just trying to eat her breakfast oatmeal.

Mom did her best to keep us seven kids fed, clean and loved. Now Eddie and I worried that we might lose our mother too and end up orphaned at our young age of sixteen. Our fears were made worse by the fact that Mom's doctors could not give her a prognosis as to what she might expect going forward.

I never asked but often wondered, *What would happen to Eddie and me if Mom died? Would we stay in the house with our sisters or be given to a relative? Our sisters would want to keep us but where would they get the money to take care of us? Dad didn't leave us any money, and Mom hardly has any money either...*

This fear drove me and Eddie to heavy binge drinking, and led us into fights with other kids on most weekends during our high school years.

One night, Eddie came home drunk, took a framed picture of Jesus Christ off the wall and began yelling, "Why? Why did you take him?" He was referring to our dad.

My mother just held him as they both cried uncontrollably.

Sadly, the alcohol use sometimes distracted my brother and me from this life lesson: life is not about avoiding suffering—it's about finding its meaning, inspiration and blessings.

Mom fought and eventually beat cancer, but she spent a lifetime fighting the demon of death. Even though Mom did not die of cancer, for all practical purposes I lost her the same day I lost my dad because she slipped into depression.

✔ Being Guided by Mentors

My intended career had been selected for me by my parents when I was in the eighth grade. In their hearts and minds, I didn't have the aptitude for regular high school. So, they let me know that I would be attending Greater New Bedford Regional Voc-Tech High School from ninth through twelfth grades, and studying Culinary Arts. My academic records undoubtedly helped in my parents' difficult decision to split up me and my twin for the very first time in our lives.

In retrospect, attending New Bedford Voc-Tech during those years was a blessing. I received the one-on-one attention I needed academically, excelled in football and developed my own identity. And to this day, I make a mean chocolate tart.

I had several high school teachers who mentored me. I recently saw my high school football coach, Mr. Constant, who told me the following story.

One day after practice, Coach Constant called us into a huddle. Evidently our performance was terrible and he needed some divine help to inspire us. The coach asked the team to bow our heads and then he began praying.

The following day after practice, Coach saw my dad walking towards him very purposefully.

"Coach," Dad said, "were you praying yesterday after practice?"

In a flash, Coach Constant saw his teaching and coaching career going down the drain. He mistakenly assumed that my Dad was upset over the team prayer and would make his feelings known to school administrators.

Coach thought about it for a few seconds and decided to just level with my father. "Yes, Mr. Caron, we were."

"Great! Keep it up." And with that, my father walked off the field.

My mentors also helped keep me out of trouble—or most of the time, anyway. There were times when not even the most inspiring, wonderful teachers and mentors could save me from the trauma I was carrying over my father's death and my mother's cancer recurrence. Sometimes this burden was more than I could handle emotionally and I acted out.

One incident in particular stands out in memory. It was after my mom's cancer recurrence, when I was a senior in high school. I turned onto my street one evening, driving too fast. I was drunk and lost control of the car, which skidded into a one-hundred-eighty-degree turn and stopped abruptly. It was a miracle that I didn't hit anyone or anything.

The New Bedford Police were right behind me, witnessed the incident, and asked to see my identification. When the officer looked at my driver's license, he recognized my last name and let me drive the fifty yards home.

"Get yourself home, and park that car!" he said.

"Okay," I said, bawling my head off.

I was an emotional mess, feeling terrible that I had embarrassed my father and brought disgrace to the Caron family name. I decided that I couldn't live with that. So, I drove myself back to the police station, drunk out of my mind, and stumbled inside. Slurring my words, I asked for the officer who had sent me home and explained that I needed to talk to him.

"What are you doing here? I told you to get to your house!" the officer said.

I cried on his shoulder, apologizing for bringing shame to my father's name.

The officer accepted my apology but pleaded for me to go directly home. "Please, go home and go to bed! I gave you a break. Now don't get me fired."

As time passed and I contemplated the life my father had led, I felt something shifting inside of me. I decided I wanted to follow in Dad's footsteps and study Criminal Justice at the local community college. So, I changed direction. I left behind my parents' plans for me to become a cook, and returned to my early childhood dream of becoming a Law Enforcement Officer.

I started taking college preparatory courses during my junior and senior years of high school. It is hard to say how much of my desire to take on the role of Law Enforcement Officer was inherent in me and how much was inspired by watching my father at work while I was growing up.

I do know that, if not for the guidance and watchful eye of wonderful teachers and mentors, I might have made mistakes that were irrevocable, and never become a Special Agent.

One of the most important father figures in my life was—and still is!—Uncle Bob. During the years following the death of my father and the recurrence of my mother's cancer, I spent many drunken evenings with Uncle Bob, crying my eyes out for my dad and trying to make sense of life.

For all intents and purposes, Uncle Bob was now my dad. As Dad's closest friend, he welcomed that role, and does so to this day. Even when he didn't have the answers, he would always have a sympathetic ear and a shoulder to cry on.

✔ Understanding the Circle of Life

I barely scraped by during college. I had very little money to buy groceries or fix my car when it overheated. My culinary arts training came in handy when there was little to eat in the house. I often ate cans of tuna fish with macaroni and cheese. That became one of my standard meals whenever I was low on cash.

Eddie would joke with me, saying, "So, what do you think we're going to have tonight, Eric?"

"Oh, I don't know," I would joke back. "How about some tuna and mac-and-cheese?"

While I was attending community college, I continued to work at St. Luke's Hospital, just as I had while attending New Bedford Voc-Tech. First, I worked as a porter in the kitchen, washing pots and pans, and then I was promoted to delivering food carts to wards, and then into a position as an orderly.

Working in a hospital, I was constantly reminded how life could change in a New York minute. I would talk to a patient one day and be transporting them to the morgue the next.

I witnessed love ones saying agonizing goodbyes, and often thought, *What if this isn't goodbye but a new journey? What if a person lives on through their relatives' eyes, hair, skin, etc.?*

We and our relatives share the same DNA, so in some very real sense this is true. If one of my relatives passes on, their DNA lives on through me. This is a very peaceful way to understand death—one that proves that dying is still living. This helped me shift my perspective. I realized that the grieving process could last a lifetime for those who don't let go and accept death.

BORN AGAIN

Beautiful butterfly joyfully free
No longer awkward or earthbound to be
The way it was changed
Tells what has happened to me

The image of the butterfly
Born again and made new
I accepted Jesus
Now I am born again too

The old me is gone
My spirit is new
The change that took place
I owe all to You

It didn't take long, an instant or so
You are with me Lord Jesus, wherever I go
The change was complete, now I am free
Made in His image, a follower I'll be

The story is not over the work incomplete
I have to tell others, whoever I meet
Accept the Lord Jesus, open your heart
Like the butterfly you will have a new start

"I tell you most solemnly unless a man is born again, he cannot see the Kingdom of God."
John 3:3

The Butterfly Card

My father always carried a Christian "butterfly" card in his wallet to remind him that we are all created as a symbol of God.

When Dad died, he had this card in his wallet and another tucked underneath his policeman's cap. An image of a butterfly is also on my dad's headstone.

In Christian art, the butterfly is often used as a symbol of hope and new beginnings, derived from the resurrection. The three distinct stages of caterpillar, chrysalis and butterfly clearly echo the cycle of life, death and resurrection. And how fitting that it is only in its triumphant final stage that the butterfly's breathtaking beauty is revealed.

A butterfly often appears in my life seemingly out of nowhere, at the perfect time and place—just when I need to know that my father is near. To this day, I carry a butterfly card in my wallet as a symbol of God wherever I go, and as a reminder that we live, die and are born again. This is the hallmark of faith.

My siblings carry butterfly cards too. And each and every time any member of the Caron clan sees a butterfly, we instantly feel our beautiful, loving dad flying around us, constantly reminding us that he is always near.

✔ The Road to Becoming a Special Agent

Once I started to gain clarity about my career path, I realized that in a way, my father's death led directly to my new path. It was a perfect example of the circle of life.

Before graduating from community college, I announced to several of my classmates that I was going on to Northeastern University (N.U.) in Boston to become a Special Agent for the U.S. Government. This way, I would still be pursuing a career as a Law Enforcement Officer like my father—but, as a Special Agent rather than a Police Officer.

There were a few smiles in the group and it was clear that no one really took me seriously. You see, Boston was a world away. And the cost of attending Northeastern? Well, let's just say it was out of my reach.

Thanks to a Massachusett law and assistance from "Uncle Jack," we Caron kids were afforded tuition-free education at any state university.

Several years after my dad's death, I had a chance to repay Uncle Jack a little bit when he asked Eddie and me to escort him to his swearing-in ceremony. It happened to be held at the auditorium of Eddie's old alma mater, New Bedford High School. Uncle Jack would have bestowed this honor on Dad but, since he wasn't around, Uncle Jack asked us Caron boys to fill in.

We dressed up in our nicest clothes and ties. Uncle Jack drove, Eddie rode shotgun and I sat in the backseat. We felt very proud to be accompanying the Mayor and we knew that Dad would have been proud of us too.

Even though Uncle Jack had come through for us in terms of college, I still had one problem: N.U. was a *private* university and my father's death benefits entitled us to attend only a state university free of charge.

I had my heart set on N.U. Their Criminal Justice program was tops in the nation, with an outstanding cooperative education program with the Federal Government. After much consideration, and encouragement and mentoring from my sister Lynn and her husband, Glenn, I applied and was accepted to N.U.

I was excited but I had my concerns. For one thing, I wasn't quite sure I could succeed academically. Then there were the student loans which weighed heavily on me. (I had to borrow twenty thousand dollars and it took me four years to repay it.)

Lastly, I wasn't sure I fit in, as the student body was primarily from a higher economic class. I recall going to Boston with my mom for a N.U. orientation. I was so excited but when we arrived to register, I had second thoughts. I saw well-dressed upper-class kids accompanied by both moms and dads, and started to feel inferior.

I wanted my dad so badly at that moment. Then, I thought, *Well, I've travelled this far, physically and emotionally, and I'm not about to turn around now!*

I just kept repeating to myself, *Come on, Dad...come on! Stay with me on this one!*

So, with my frail mom on my arm, we walked into a packed auditorium and I never looked back.

✔ Following in My Father's Footsteps

The summer before I started school at N.U., I applied for and was offered a position with the Wareham, Massachusetts Police Department as a Summer Police Officer.

I thought it would be good experience for my future career. More importantly, I figured I might have a tough road ahead of me in landing a Special Agent job. So, I wanted to have a backup plan, just in case. Becoming a Police Officer was my Plan B.

I was excited to wear the badge and uniform and serve just like my dad. I was just shy of twenty-one years old and not yet even legal to drink alcohol in Massachusetts. (That's not to say I *didn't* drink...only that I wasn't yet legal to drink.)

Wareham is the gateway to Cape Cod. It sits at the head of beautiful Buzzards Bay with its fifty-seven miles of lovely coastline and beautiful beaches. During the summer months, its population doubles, thanks to the arrival of tourists who prefer to avoid the Cape traffic and bridges.

After an abbreviated stint at the Police Academy that lasted several weeks and covered criminal law, motor vehicle law, arrest techniques, the use of deadly force and other basic topics, the department held a small swearing-in ceremony.

At the graduation ceremony, Mom was very proud to see me in uniform and told all the brass that I was following in my father's footsteps.

I also felt Dad standing alongside me as I took the oath of office as he had done some thirty years earlier. I felt him grinning from ear to ear.

I thought, *Oh, how I wish he was here...not for me but for Mom who is standing all alone with tears in her eyes.*

✔ Wearing the Police Badge and Uniform

At the end of Academy training, I started taking an honest inventory of myself in light of the responsibilities that went along with being a Summer Police Officer. That's when a disturbing thought came to me:

I may actually be required to take a life based on the totality of the circumstances!

I found myself rehearsing potential scenarios. I wondered, *What if a man has a gun pointed at me and fails to drop it? Would I have to shoot him? Or what if he comes at me with a knife or a baseball bat? What would I do then?*

The responsibilities that came with the position weighed heavily on this twenty-year-old. Wearing the uniform began to make me feel much like a superhero, expected to perform life-threatening and life-saving feats at any given moment. It didn't take long for me to realize I was profoundly uncomfortable in this role.

I started to sense that I was not Police Officer material even before a series of on-the-job bungles that drove home the point. The first occurred one day as I was directing traffic in and out of a restaurant onto Route 6.

I thought, *Directing traffic? Piece of cake. What could go wrong?*

As I was directing traffic, I noticed an elderly woman driving out of the restaurant. She was wearing a neck brace, and it was clearly having a negative impact on her ability to drive safely. In fact, she was struggling to look left and right as she pulled onto the busy roadway.

I approached her and simply said, "Ma'am, you really shouldn't be driving with that brace on your neck! Your range of motion is limited and you may cause an accident."

She started loudly explaining that her doctor had told her that she was fit to drive. She was so defensive, you would have thought I'd written her a hundred-dollar ticket.

I listened and then repeated what I had told her the first time—that I didn't feel she was in any shape to be driving.

Fifteen minutes later, I was visited by a Sergeant who told me that the neck-brace lady had gone to the station and complained about me. I couldn't decide whether I was more annoyed with the lady or the Sergeant who actually took the time to come speak to me.

I couldn't believe I had already received my first police-harassment complaint over a routine non-event where I was just trying to prevent an accident. I can only imagine what would have happened if I had actually given that lady a ticket. This was another lightbulb moment for me and helped lead me to the certainty that police work was not my path.

The next incident that helped cement that realization involved an equally routine assignment.

The Summer Police Officers spent most days walking busy tourist areas. One evening, I had a 4:00 p.m.—midnight assignment patrolling Wareham Main Street on foot. Around 9:00 p.m., I was asked via radio to call the station. Some police calls needed to be conducted over a phone because of possible listening ears on the police radio. This was prior to the proliferation of cell phones, but payphones were positioned throughout the town and that's what I used to make the call.

After I made the call, I continued my shift. Suddenly I realized I hadn't heard any police chatter on my portable police radio in a while. Then I realized I didn't actually *have* my portable police radio. I seemed to have lost it. I couldn't believe it.

I hurried back to the pay phone I had used to call the station, and to the restaurant where I had stopped to eat dinner. No luck.

Well, I said to myself, *I sure had a short police career, lasting all of a month!* I felt like Barney Fife from the classic T.V. series, *The Andy Griffith Show.*

As I sat at the police station, typing up the report about my missing radio, I was embarrassed beyond words.

The Sergeant, on the other hand, was professional, sympathetic and optimistic that the radio would reappear. This was the same Sergeant who had reprimanded me. He was a father figure who gave me a kick in the ass when I needed one but also showed me a little loving kindness to keep me encouraged. It was exactly what my own father used to do.

✔ Confirmation that I Wanted to be a Special Agent

As I drove home that night, I had the confirmation I needed—becoming a Police Officer was not for me. I was more determined than ever to become a Special Agent.

Well, I guess I won't have the luxury of a Plan B, I said to myself. *So, Plan A better work out!*

I had a restless night of sleep, knowing I had lost my police radio. In the morning, I was awakened by my mother, telling me that the Sergeant was on the house phone.

I sprang to my feet and rushed to the phone. I was incredibly relieved to hear that a man had discovered my portable radio at the pay phone and brought it to the police station. I had no idea why the man waited a full day to return the radio but I was glad it had reappeared.

Here was the final incident that convinced me that I was more suited for a career as a Special Agent than a Police Officer. It was the Fourth of July and most of the Wareham Police Department resources were concentrated on the celebration.

I was given a neighborhood walking patrol assignment, no doubt as a result of my lost radio incident of a few weeks earlier. I said to myself, *I'm sure the brass wants me nowhere near any potential action.*

It was about 7:30 in the evening and, as I was walking, I heard yelling off in the distance. As I came around a street corner, I saw two males and two females fighting in the front yard of a home. I hustled up the driveway, announcing my presence, thinking that would put an end to the fight. Unfortunately, it only further agitated one of the males who picked up a large fence pole and started swinging it at the other guy.

I said to myself, *Boy, so much for a peaceful night away from any action!*

I immediately took out my baton and got between the two males. I yelled at the man to drop the pole but he refused. I hesitated, asking myself, *Do I strike him with my baton? Do I shoot him?*

A three-way standoff followed, with escalating tension between the two bad guys, and me stuck in the middle. I had no idea what the right next steps should be. I was paralyzed with fear and completely stuck. I decided to call for assistance and an ambulance.

It was a good thing I had thought to call for an ambulance. One of the females was now on the ground, crying in pain. She'd gotten hit by something—what, I didn't know. She ended up being transported to the hospital by ambulance.

I had radioed for backup but in all the commotion, I failed to hear the station radio transmitting back to me. When I didn't respond, they feared that I was in the midst of a serious situation, and sent the entire station to back me up.

Suddenly, I saw all these police cruisers headed my way. They just kept coming. That's when I realized, *Oh, no…looks like I might have given them the impression that things here are worse than they actually are!*

By the time the multitude of police officers showed up, it was clear that the situation was tense but by no means catastrophic. It certainly didn't warrant the presence of the entire station.

So, some of the guys were giving me the evil eye. Understandably, they felt like, "What the hell? You could have told us everything was under control! We thought you were dead!"

I felt like such a schmuck. At the same time, I was glad it had happened. Between the neck-brace lady, losing my police radio and this incident, I had all the evidence I needed to solve the mystery of whether or not becoming a Police Officer was a viable Plan B.

✔ Learning from My Experiences

I had spent three long months as a Police Officer—a stint that included, along with the incidents mentioned here, issuing parking tickets to angry citizens, breaking up barroom fights, and attending to motor vehicle accidents. I was done.

Three wonderful blessings had come from my summer job. First of all, I developed an even deeper appreciation of the men and women who wear the police uniform and strap on a gun and badge every day as they go to work.

As a boy, I always idolized my Police Officer father, but it was only when I wore that uniform, badge and gun myself that I truly understood the selflessness and sacrifice entailed in that particular calling. On any given day, at any moment, a Police Officer may be asked to sacrifice his or her life for someone with whom they have no blood ties.

On top of that, a Police Officer may be asked—or even compelled by law!—to explain their on-the-job actions to the community or the courts, and suffer through being judged by those who have the benefit of time and videotape as they scrutinize every split-second decision made by the officer.

Secondly, being a Summer Police Officer taught me the importance of listening to myself and my instincts, assessing situations quickly and instinctively, and taking appropriate action. Many people fail to absorb data from their environment—and the ones who do receive and assess it often fail to take action. They are not switched on.

My experiences that summer were rich with lessons and wisdom. I learned from every person I encountered or met, every driver I stopped, every call I went on and every talk I had with my fellow Police Officers. All of it led me to a deeper understanding of myself, police work and human nature.

Taking all of that into consideration, I was able to make an informed decision about who I was as a person, what my strengths were and were not, and the aspects of the job I did and did not enjoy doing. I found that the day-to-day duties that went along with being a Police Officer definitely did not appeal to me or make my heart sing. As I listened to myself and my instincts, my father was there with internal guidance.

Finally, my summer job helped me clarify and narrow down my career ambitions. Now more than ever, I had my heart set on becoming a Special Agent for the U.S. Government. I was so thankful to the Wareham Police Department for giving me the opportunity and experience, but I was now on my way to Northeastern University to pursue my dream.

As I moved forward on my career path, I had my father very much on my mind and in my heart. I also kept a special place in my heart for the countless men and women who choose to make police work their life's work.

✔ Remembering What Dad Had Taught Me

While at Northeastern, I made the hour-and-a-half drive each way from New Bedford in my Toyota Tercel that occasionally overheated on the expressway. Sometimes I hopped a ride with friends. Worst case scenario, I took the bus up and back.

I made it onto the Dean's List several times and was interviewed and selected as an intern with the Department of Treasury, U.S. Customs Service, Office of Investigations, Washington, D.C. Another hurdle behind me.

One class I took at N.U. turned out to be a godsend in the way it impacted my alcohol use. It was a nutrition course, an easy three-credit course that may have saved my life. During the course, there was a practical exercise: for an entire weekend, I was required to document all food and liquid intake. This was designed to make us take stock of what we were putting into our mouths, and in what quantities.

Well, on one Friday night, I drank fifteen beers and six vodka shots. Seeing those numbers on a graph was shocking. This nutrition course drove home the SEE philosophy instilled in me by my father. I was reminded of the importance of sleeping eight hours a night, eating right and exercising. Drinking too much did not fit into the SEE philosophy at all.

Remembering what Dad had taught me, and recommitting myself to SEE helped me give up my habit of drinking too much alcohol. This brought about a big shift in my life for the better, and not a moment too soon. I was going to need to be switched on for my schoolwork, and switched on when I actually became a Special Agent. Alcohol had no real place in that scenario.

✔ Starting a New Chapter of My Life

In October of 1987, my mom came home from getting her hair cut and started describing her new beautician as a very lovely Portuguese girl.

I said, half-jokingly, "Great! Why don't you ask her out for me?"

Well, during her next appointment she did.

So, at twenty-one, I met my wife, Marie. She was a first-generation immigrant from Portugal. She arrived with her parents and two younger sisters at Logan Airport in 1977 with a hundred dollars in their pockets. That money was quickly used for the fifty-five-mile taxi ride to New Bedford, Massachusetts where the family made their home in a three-tenement (a three-level house where each floor is rented out as a separate apartment).

As the oldest, Marie grew up taking care of her sisters while both her parents worked. She spent her summers attending summer school to learn English. She was quiet but adventurous and determined to live a better life. I was too.

I knew there was something special about her. Besides being beautiful, she was smart, a survivor and had an impeccable work ethic. She would become the yin in our relationship. She taught me that the combination of yoga, meditation and proper nutrition was the foundation for a peaceful life. (This was similar to the SEE philosophy, so it made sense to me.)

Marie financially supported me during my final years at college, and until I began earning money as a Special Agent.

Now I had the woman of my dreams in my life. And I was about to start down a career path I'd looked forward to ever since I was a little guy listening to the police scanner and chasing the fire trucks and police vehicles to their calls.

On New Year's Day of 1988, at 6:00 am, I said goodbye to my mother and Marie and set off on a cold New England morning to greet my future. Eddie was coming with me. We were leaving New Bedford so I could start my internship with the U.S. Government, and we were both excited about the journey.

We were making the trip without cell phones or a GPS, both of which were still years in the future. As we began our nine-hour drive from New Bedford to Washington, D.C., we got about two miles down the road when disaster struck. The hood of my Toyota Tercel flew up to my windshield and I couldn't see a damned thing.

Thankfully, God was watching out for us. Even though it was still early in the morning, we found an open auto-repair shop and a mechanic who helped us secure the hood.

We arrived in D.C. with only a hundred dollars in our pockets (much like Marie's family had done upon arriving in New Bedford). After two weeks of living on my old standby of canned tuna and mac-and-cheese, I finally got a paycheck. To celebrate, I used my culinary skills and prepared a nice steak dinner for my brother and me.

Eddie had accompanied me on the first leg of my journey and now it was his turn to pursue his dream of becoming a football coach. He flew back to Massachusetts and headed to Springfield College. Football was my brother's life. He was a football captain while attending New Bedford High School and played both sides of the line. He led the team in tackles, and was the highest graded player on the defense chart.

✔ Taking Dad with Me

I began to settle into my new job as an intern, working in the National Security Division of United States Customs (now called Customs & Border Protection), assisting senior desk agents who managed worldwide covert arms cases.

As a young intern, I often jogged the mall in Washington, D.C. My father had spent time there, playing with the Marine Corps Band. With the Capitol on one end, the Lincoln Memorial on the other, and the Washington Monument and military memorials in between, I was truly inspired.

I would spend most runs talking with my dad about all the amazing historical sites. I would often tear up just at the thought of him.

Look, Dad! I would say out loud. *I'm in Washington! I'm going to be that agent you always wanted to be.*

My dad had always wanted to be a Special Agent himself, but he never got the education or opportunities I got in life.

In January, 1989, I successfully fulfilled my degree requirements and completed two six-month intern assignments with the government. Now it was time to work the phones and get an agent interview.

In April, 1989 after several failed attempts, I got an interview with the Special Agent in Charge, Newark, New Jersey. I had no idea where Newark was, and had never even heard of the city—but I really didn't care. This was my opportunity to become a Special Agent.

I spent days preparing for the interview and Marie purchased my first business suit. We travelled to New Jersey together and she stayed in the car as I went into the office. After two hours, I came out and was met by a sign that simply said, "Congratulations!" Somehow, Marie knew I would get the job.

That summer, after years of struggles and sheer determination, I became a Special Agent, U.S. Customs, Newark, New Jersey. I was sworn in pending my graduation from the training academy and told that, if I were to fail more than one test during training, I would flunk out and lose my status as a Special Agent.

I spent the next eighteen-plus weeks of intense physical and academic training, including firearms and tactical training at the Federal Law Enforcement Training Center in Glynco, Georgia.

✔ Becoming a Special Agent at Last

In October of 1989, on a day witnessed by Mom and Marie, I graduated. It was a triumphant day, but one also filled with tears and sadness as I looked out into the crowd and missed my dad.

I had fulfilled my dad's dreams. Now it was time for me to perform. I returned home to pack up my car. Time to move to my four-hundred-dollar-a-month apartment in Bayonne, New Jersey.

Bayonne was a town where the homes were so close together, you could pass toothpaste out the bathroom window to your neighbor. It was a notorious organized-crime town. Violent street crime was virtually non-existent there because organized crime ran the town and people in general were afraid of stepping on the toes of the crime bosses.

Marie and I were not yet married but we wanted to spend as much time together as possible. So, the plan was that I would work all week in New Jersey and, on Friday evenings, brave the New York/Connecticut traffic to make the four-to-six-hour drive to her parents' home in Fairhaven, Massachusetts. Then, on Mondays at 3:00 in the morning, I would get back in the car and commute in the opposite direction, and try to make it to my desk by 8:30 a.m.

I gave my mom a hug while she stood on the front porch. She couldn't walk down the stairs that day because of the arthritis in her knees so the porch was as far as she could go.

Saying goodbye to me, Mom began to cry. "I'm so proud of you, Eric! I just wish your father was here!"

"He is here, Mom. He's in me."

That resonated with her because I look very much like my dad.

I made the five-hour trip south, reliving my life—the good and not so good. As I drove, I dreamed of returning home to New Bedford one day as a Special Agent to lead an operation that would be covered by the worldwide media.

✔ Reporting for Duty

On November 2nd, 1989, I reported for duty. I was assigned to Newark, the Renaissance City, as it was referred to on the signage that greeted you as you entered the city. Every time, I saw that sign, I chuckled to myself.

As I said, Newark at that time was a dump with the highest crime rate in the state. From a violence standpoint, it was truly the Wild, Wild West of the East Coast. Going out to your car at the end of a long day was hair-raising. You never knew what you might encounter.

Our government-issued vehicles were stolen weekly. It got so bad, we had to put lock-bars on our steering wheels. On several occasions, we had chases and shootouts. We even had one agent who surprised a thief who was trying to steal his car. The agent nearly got run over by the thief while he was trying to get away.

My squad was filled with seasoned Special Agents. They were all great guys who had my back on the streets during surveillance, arrests and search warrants. They cursed like typical New Yorkers and some of them smoked in the office. And, of course, there was plenty of beer and wine flowing at our festive holiday office parties.

My drug squad was "running and gunning" with multiple cases involving thousands of kilos of cocaine being imported from South America (mainly Colombia). Sometimes, we were reacting to a call at a seaport where an informant or Customs Inspector was calling to say, "We just discovered multiple kilos of heroin and cocaine in a shipment."

The squad then had to get our search warrant and equipment, along with all the tools we needed to do our jobs, and rush out the door to set up at the location.

On other days, we were running out the door on proactive cases. These were long-term investigations with a specific target, where we were building a dossier on the target. We would collect the target's trash and mail, follow him and identify his associates. We might have an informant providing intelligence on the target, and that informant might introduce an Undercover Special Agent (UCA) to the target.

In my entire career as a Special Agent, I never stepped into the role of Undercover Special Agent for any length of time. Given the type of person I am, being a UCA is not in my DNA. Here's why: I am a terrible liar—a good trait to carry into real life, but a liability that could cost lives in deep undercover work.

Not only does a UCA need to be a convincing liar but they also need to have great emotional dexterity as they switch effortlessly back and forth between two different roles. They have to convincingly wear their disguise as a bad guy, making sure they look and play the part one hundred percent at every minute. And they also have to constantly think like an agent, stay alert and aware of everything they say, and keep in mind the kind of evidence they will need for court. There are always a lot of moving parts in any operation.

✔ Devastated by Another Loss

On December 19th, 1989, I received an urgent page to call sector, our communication facility. When I called, they said I had an urgent call from Marie and told me to please call her right away.

When I called Marie, she was crying uncontrollably. Her youngest sister Alice had just been killed in a motor vehicle accident. She was only twenty-one years old at the time.

I hadn't spent much time with Alice and didn't know her well at all. She was living away from home by the time I met Marie, so we hadn't had much of a chance to bond. Still, I was in shock and terribly upset.

I couldn't believe we were losing Marie's sister only one week before Christmas. Not only was Christmas upon us, but I had been planning to pick up an engagement ring I had made for Marie and ask her to marry me.

Marie was absolutely devastated, of course, along with her mom, dad and sister. I was committed to being strong and supportive for Marie and her family and knew I needed to take time off work.

I called my supervisor to let him know what was going on. I told him I would be heading north to Massachusetts and would be out of the office for a week. Before making the long drive, I had to go to Staten Island to pick up the engagement ring for Marie. It was eight o'clock at night when I called the jeweler.

He promised to stay late and work on the ring until it was finished. It was midnight by the time I put the ring in my pocket and got on the road. It took nearly five hours to travel to Massachusetts. By the time I arrived, the sun was coming up.

✔ Getting Engaged in the Midst of Tragedy

Within twenty-four hours of Alice's death, I proposed to Marie at her parents' house in her childhood bedroom. We were sitting on the floor of her room, and we were both in tears with grief over her sister.

I wanted to bring some joy and happiness into Marie's life, and I had already planned to ask her to marry me. So, I said I had something to give her, something I had planned on presenting to her on Christmas. I said I thought she needed a little extra love at that moment. (It was a few days before Christmas).

She was elated but grief-stricken over her sister. It was strange to be getting engaged while she was so devastated.

Because of the holiday, the funeral services weren't held until after Christmas. The wake was attended by hundreds of Alice's friends and family members and the mass was held the day after Christmas. The loss of a twenty-one-year-old was devastating, and it was brutal to be saying goodbye at Christmastime. Talk about a Blue Christmas!

Within months of presenting Marie with her engagement ring, I was surprised with a treasured ring of my own. In 1990, while coaching at Cornell University, Eddie's football team won the Ivy League Championship.

One evening shortly afterwards, Eddie invited me and Marie to join him and his fiancé, Judy, at a restaurant for dinner. Eddie was proudly wearing his championship ring.

We spoke about our dad and how proud he would have been of our achievements thus far in life. Then, at the end of our meal we ordered dessert. When the chocolate cake came, it had a little extra love in it. Eddie had scraped together enough money to buy me a duplicate championship ring, and presented it to me on a silver platter with the dessert. It was a symbol of his love for me.

During my entire year-long engagement with Marie, I travelled back and forth each weekend to see her. Then, on April 29th, 1990 we were married in a small Catholic Church in Fairhaven, Massachusetts.

Eddie was my best man and Marie's surviving sister, Fatima, was her maid of honor. We were married by Father Tom, one of the priests from my father's funeral. We had become good friends and he mentored Marie and me and held our hands through the sacrament of marriage.

It was a bittersweet day. We were both grief-stricken—her without her sister Alice at the wedding, and me without my dad. The reception was as festive as it could be under the circumstances. It was arranged by an event production company with their own indoor facility, and we had an overflowing traditional, delicious Portuguese feast.

As a new Special Agent and a newlywed, I would seldom see my wife. Between my job and Marie's new job with Continental Airlines as an International Sales Agent, we were often like two ships passing in the night. I spent more time sleeping in my G-ride while on various operations than I did with her.

✔ Protecting the President

In 1991 and 1992, I was selected (along with other Special Agents) to assist the Secret Service during the George H.W. Bush/Bill Clinton Presidential Campaign. I had always thought the activities of the Secret Service seemed so glamorous and mysterious until I actually got assigned to Secret Service detail.

The assignment involved travelling for twenty-one days on the road in seven-day-a-week, twelve-hour shifts. Despite being assigned to the presidential campaign, I never even got to meet either of the presidential candidates.

Here's why: there were various levels of agents on any Secret Service detail. The agents on the protective detail were on the inner perimeter and they traveled with the "protectee." The other agents—some of whom were Secret Service Agents, and some of whom were agents from Treasury, A.T.F., U.S. Customs, or I.R.S.—were the B-team, so to speak. That was my role.

Those of us on the B-team supported the A-team agents. For example, they might let us know, "We need five agents on the hotel door…at the hospital…stationed in the hotel…in the lobby…in the kitchen."

If we were lucky, the presidential motorcade might drive past us and we'd get a glimpse of the president, but there was no guarantee. After all, we were not on the inner perimeter.

I did get to meet Barbara Bush during a visit to New Jersey. She was very humble and not at all holier-than-thou or pretentious. Her daughters had the same kind, humble demeanor. Due to my intimate proximity to the protectee, I would see and hear a lot and get to know the real person. That was one satisfying aspect of Secret Service work— getting to see the protectee in a relaxed setting, away from cameras and the press.

During my years as a Special Agent, I would also work protection assignments at the U.N. General Assembly. Once a year, the United Nations holds their assembly, and all foreign heads of state attend. It's a prime target for terrorism because you have approximately one hundred and eighty heads of state, all requiring protection. So, they pulled the B-team agents to work with the Secret Service guys.

Whenever I was covering a foreign protectee, I was interacting with their protection detail as well, and working in partnership with them. I needed to be as professional as possible, given that I was representing the U.S. Government. Regardless of whether the protectee was foreign or domestic, the same principles applied in terms of being switched on at all times.

Years after the Bush/Clinton campaign, when Pat Buchanan ran for president, I was again on the Secret Service B-team. There were several of us agents assigned to guard his residence. All we had to do was monitor the cameras and alarms at his house and keep an eye out for intruders. Talk about being on the outer perimeter.

I spent twenty-one, twelve-hour days watching Buchanan's house. This was a cushy assignment, especially when the protectee was on the road—but living out of a suitcase and eating dinner out every night got old very quickly.

One funny incident occurred on that Pat Buchanan assignment. Someone had noticed that the water level in the pool in Buchanan's backyard was low. So, they stuck a hose in the pool to let it slowly fill up.

"Hey, do us a favor," one of the agents from the A-team said to me. "Shut the hose off when the pool is full."

"Sure, no problem," I said and promptly forgot about it.

Eight hours later, the water was overflowing into the yard and I was confronted with falling down on the job.

"You forgot to shut the water off?" they asked me, incredulously.

Thankfully, the water did not flood the house.

The Secret Service assignment lasted just long enough for me to thank God that it wasn't my full-time career. My true passion at the time was international drug smuggling investigations.

✔ Riding the Wave Between Boredom and Terror

The general public has this perception that the Secret Service is secret, and that's true everywhere but the United States. In most countries when you say Secret Service, it refers to their intelligence agencies, like our C.I.A.

When it comes to *our* Secret Service, their investigations are limited in scope and deal mostly with protecting the president, the vice president and others covered by law. That is their primary mission. Their secondary mission is to investigate counterfeiting of credit cards and U.S. currency.

Secret Service work entails days and days of boredom interspersed with seconds of terror when there's an attempt on your protectee's life. You're either bored to death or scared to death.

It's mind-numbingly boring to stand at a post for hours, guarding a protectee. During all the hours you're standing there, you have to be switched on because the weakest link in the perimeter could invite an attack. So even if you're blocks away from the actual event, or stationed in the kitchen of the event venue, you still have to be switched on, paying attention.

You may only be on the second or third perimeter of an event, but if someone who is not properly credentialed gets through your layer of security because you failed to be switched on and weren't paying proper attention, it's your fault, you're responsible, and you've invited an attack.

Unfortunately, if a bad guy gets through the various layers of security and makes their way to a protectee, it usually happens without any of the agents knowing until the bad guy has made contact with the protectee. Only later, during a follow-up investigation of an incident, when every step of the bad guy is being retraced, is it discovered which layer of the security perimeter was breached.

Any time there is an attempt on a protectee's life, it means there was a breakdown in security. For example, while President Reagan was still in office, John Hinckley, Jr. managed to find his way into the press pool. Once inside, he attempted to assassinate President Reagan. He was able to shoot the president near his heart, and permanently disable the president's assistant and White House Press Secretary, James Brady.

During the era when President Reagan and James Brady were shot, there was no Special Agent assigned to make sure the press was credentialed. There is now, due in no small part to that shooting.

Then there was the incident that occurred with President Ronald Reagan sometime after he had left office. The former president was onstage in California giving a presentation when a bad guy appeared onstage and crept up on him from behind.

The Secret Service got to the bad guy within seconds and there was a minor altercation onstage between the Secret Service Agents and the bad guy. The fact that the bad guy was able to get so close to the president tells us that a total breakdown occurred at one or more levels of the security perimeter.

Both Hinckley and the bad guy that approached President Reagan while he was speaking onstage after he had left office penetrated multiple layers of security. Any time there's an attempt to gain access to a protectee, there's a weak link someplace. That's the rule of thumb.

✔ Surveilling the Drug Smugglers

O ne particular case from early June of 1991 will haunt me forever. The case involved six so-called importers, responsible for transporting over a thousand kilos of cocaine via a shipping container that arrived in New York. The criminals were using an organized crime member's business as the front company or importer.

After the Customs Inspectors discovered the load, my group effected a controlled delivery to the importer's place of business in Brooklyn. This was accomplished by inserting one of our Undercover Special Agents ("a UCA") as the driver. Then a team of agents covertly followed the container with air support. Meanwhile, tech agents were able to place a trip wire on the container door and listening devices inside the packages of soap in which the kilos of cocaine were hidden.

Ideally, we preferred to replace a live load (actual drugs) with a fake load (sham). We didn't always have that luxury. From the moment of importation, time was of the essence. We could only stall and blow smoke for so long before the bad guys caught on.

They knew what was inside their shipments and any hesitation on our part to receive a shipment would raise an eyebrow or two. Our very lives depended upon our ability to keep a poker face. If we were to let a target know that they were under suspicion, it could blow an entire case.

When we did have time to replace the live load with sham, we would replace ninety-nine percent of the drugs. We always left a trace of the real drugs to prove our case later in court. When our window of opportunity to replace the load was closed, unfortunately we had no choice but to go with a live load. That's what happened in this case.

Once the container had been delivered, the organized crime target (the president of the front company importing the goods) was seen leaving the business. He started driving around the block. It was obvious that he was "hinky." (We agents used the word hinky to describe all sorts of activities of bad guys. It was a way of saying that he was nervous, squirrely and anxious.)

That first night, the wires didn't pick up any activity. So, a decision was made to do a covert break-in to make sure the cocaine was still inside and the wires were working. A decision was also made *not* to inform the NYPD this early into the case.

We had two reasons for keeping it to ourselves for the moment. First, we didn't want the interference. And secondly, we couldn't be certain that the target didn't have influence over certain police officials. That is always a possibility.

Sometimes it's not an issue of the Police Officer being deep in the pockets of the bad guy. It could also be that we're simply worried about loose lips. We always want to prevent a Police Officer from saying something that could be overheard like, "Hey, did you hear that the feds came in today? They're looking at Joey down the street."

So, we had the police on a need-to-know basis. We would read them into the case at some point but definitely not early, early on.

After setting up a perimeter, I and fellow agents made our way over the barbed wire. I hate heights—a trait I might have picked up when my mother got so frightened over finding me as a little tyke, wandering out on the bulkhead. So, I gladly stayed on the ground.

The tech agent and several other agents made their way to the roof. The team on the roof opened the ventilation hatch, made their way down and immediately shut off any alarms. Then they opened a door for me and the rest of the team.

We discovered that the cocaine was still in place and the tech equipment still active. After approximately thirty minutes inside, we left. Mission accomplished.

Days later, the president of the front company came forward and flipped on the importers. He said, "I know you're onto me. I want to cooperate."

So, how did he get wise to us? We may never know for sure. He may have had a source inside the Police Department. It was also conceivable that his gut told him that something was up.

I was a team member rather than the case agent so I never found out how he figured out that we were onto him. From a security standpoint, certain things are revealed only on a need-to-know basis, even within the group working the case.

We might have needed to know, for example, if the target had been alerted to us due to some breach on our part. In such an event, the case agent might come to us and say something like, "Hey, the target made the surveillance because you were following too close!"

Interestingly, the target confessed that coming forward and turning himself in was actually Plan B.

Plan A was: "Screw this! I'm going to burn the place down and destroy the evidence." He had already thrown his weapon into the East River while we were secretly inside the warehouse.

Luckily for us, he had a change of heart. I will always wonder what changed his mind.

Getting caught for a major crime is like a game of tag. He knew he was "it" and that his only hope for reducing his sentence was to tag someone else for us. He was ready to assist us by swapping in one of our UCAs in place of one of his guys.

✔ Taking Down the Importers

Here's how the illegal importation operation worked. Six foreign nationals (Cubans and Panamanians) organized the exportation from Colombia, got the drugs on a vessel, and made the arrangements for the shipment to be delivered into the U.S. They conspired with "Tony" the organized crime guy to utilize his company as a front to receive the drugs. Once the drugs had been received by Tony, they now needed to be returned to the foreign nationals.

It all went like clockwork. Tony introduced our UCA (who was wired with a listening device) to the smugglers as his rep. The agent flashed a sample of the cocaine load. The smugglers negotiated cost with the agent and agreed to the logistics of when and how the entire shipment of drugs would be received.

Meanwhile, once I and my fellow agents got the incriminating talk we needed to proceed with a takedown, we followed the importers back to their Newark Hotel. As they entered the lobby, we tackled them with our guns drawn, taking down three of them at gunpoint—with tourists walking by. That was a dicey operation but just another day in Newark, New Jersey.

Now we had three of the six foreign nationals. Meanwhile, other agents took down the other three smugglers. Several of the six smugglers, realizing they were now "it," cooperated. They continued the game of tag, agreeing to introduce a UCA who would make the U.S. sales to various distributors in the New York region. These distributors were the bosses of the street drug dealers, and responsible for orchestrating the dissemination of the drugs throughout the East Coast.

✔ Making a Fatal Mistake

My supervisor instructed me to obtain kilos of sham cocaine for the scheduled meetings. So, I quickly drove to the warehouse in New Jersey and located the shipping container that the sham kilos were in. This was government stash used for the purpose of operations.

Unfortunately, I couldn't locate the sham bags quickly enough because they weren't marked and had been thrown into a shipping container with bags of potatoes. I knew I did not have enough time to find the sham and get back in time for the scheduled meetings.

So, I called my supervisor and updated him on the time crunch.

This particular manager had limited street experience and would always ask junior agents, "What should we do?" or "What do you think?" during an operation.

When he asked what we should do, I said, "You'll have to go with a live load."

My supervisor agreed with my suggestion.

Then I asked, "What time is the operational briefing?"

"We have no time for a briefing, so just get back and set up in the area."

We had multiple meetings established. There was going to be a 1:00 p.m. meeting with one set of bad guys, and an hour later, more bad guys would be showing up for more kilos. With the first set of bad guys showing up in an hour, my supervisor felt that there was no time for a briefing.

When the supervisor stated that we didn't have time for an operational briefing, it hit me right in the gut. I knew that letting the bad guys dictate our pace and compromise our security was a potentially fatal mistake. Skipping an operational briefing goes against all basic rules of thumb. You always brief before you go out and play. It was the cardinal rule.

Even in a concert or a play where the stakes are very low, the players rehearse so everyone knows their part in the performance and it doesn't fall apart on stage. In my line of work where lives were at stake, it was all the more important that we had a plan, and that everyone was briefed on the plan before being thrown on the street to fly blind.

What are we doing here? I asked myself. *This is f***ed up... ludicrous...crazy!*

I didn't know how to say, "F**k that, guys! Let's stop this operation until we can have a briefing!"

I was on a conveyer belt with all these other agents. Unfortunately, it was moving so fast beneath my feet, I didn't have time to hop off so I could go sit on a rock somewhere and come up with the best course of action.

Between our agency and the DEA, we had about fifty agents on the streets. I told myself, *Well, every one of these agents and all their supervisors have signed onto this! What am I going to do? Put an end to it? Somebody above me should catch this!*

If I had been a seasoned agent (instead of a new one), and switched on, I would have spoken to the case agent and other senior agents and insisted upon a proper briefing. I would have said, "This is ludicrous, going out there without a real briefing! It goes against all protocol, training, experience and common sense."

The case agent reported directly to the supervisor who decided that we didn't need a proper briefing. He could have said to his supervisor,

"I have spoken to Eric and I am not comfortable proceeding without a proper briefing."

Being a junior agent, I saluted and said, "Yes, sir!" That's something I'll have to live with for the rest of my life.

✔ Flying Blind

We were thrown out on the street with only an ad hoc briefing and told about our assignments. I was told to get into the area and set up.

My gut was warning me against inserting myself into an arena where I did not know who the players were, or who was going to do what, and when. I knew that when the bullets started flying, it was anybody's guess who was going to get hit. I wanted to stay blocks away from that, and I did. The meeting location was a hotel parking lot close to our office but I set up offstage, a few blocks away.

The UCA, John, gave the bust signal—the closing of the trunk which had been opened to show that the drugs were inside. The bust team moved in for the arrest. In the heat of the takedown, the UCA, who was still on scene and standing between the two bad guys, was shot in the back.

I could hear over the radio that something had gone terribly wrong. As I exited my G-Ride, I saw the UCA on the ground, screaming in pain. Meanwhile, the bad guys were getting their asses kicked on the hood of another G-Ride. The agents were tearing off the bad guys' clothes, looking for the gun that was used to shoot the UCA.

It never occurred to them that the bullet might have come from a colleague's gun. Yet, that was exactly what had happened—the agent was shot by friendly fire from the supervisor-driver. (The accidental discharge was captured on our guys' surveillance video.)

After a few minutes of watching the other agents search the bad guys for the weapon that shot John, the inexperienced supervisor-driver admitted to accidentally discharging his weapon. He would end up getting transferred to Washington, D.C. to Headquarters where he was assigned to a desk job for a couple of years. That was the only disciplinary action taken—a paid transfer to Washington, D.C.

While the other agents secured the scene, I decided to follow the ambulance to the hospital. At the time, I had no specific reason for doing so. In hindsight, I believe I just wanted to be away from the shooting scene.

As I drove to the hospital, I called my wife to give her the terrible news.

Marie asked, "He had his bulletproof vest on, right?"

My wife always reminded me to wear mine when I was out "playing" (arresting bad guys).

"Sadly, no, he wasn't," I said.

Unfortunately, sometimes Undercover Special Agents don't wear bulletproof vests because they're worried about being searched and having their cover blown. Any UCA who does choose to wear his vest is rolling the dice. He has to decide if he's ready to answer some hard questions if he gets caught wearing it.

He could always say, "I'm no f**king cop but I don't know who *you* are! So, yeah, I'm wearing a f**king vest!" But there's no way of knowing whether such a statement would fly.

As John was rushed into the E.R., I had a chance to speak to the medic. Unfortunately, the information I got from the medic was devastating: he believed that John would likely be paralyzed for life. Sadly, he would turn out to be correct.

While I was at the hospital, I saw John's family arrive and I witnessed their tears and anguish over discovering the condition of their loved one and his sad prognosis. Their pain is forever engraved in my mind and heart.

The next day, another agent and I went to the county jail and picked up the two bad guys who were arrested the previous day in the takedown. They needed to be processed at our office and then brought to Federal Court for their initial appearance.

They were both in pretty bad shape from resisting arrest and being roughed up during the arrest by agents who mistakenly believed that one of them was concealing the weapon used to shoot John.

I slammed one of the handcuffed bad guys against the wall, saying, "If not for you bastards, my friend would still be walking!"

It killed me to know that, if only these bad guys hadn't ordered up the cocaine, John would still be walking around instead of spending the rest of his life in a wheelchair.

Days after the shooting, a counselor was brought in to speak to us. His philosophy, and that of some of the managers, was: "You've fallen off the horse. It's best to just get back on and keep riding. Get back to work."

The unspoken message was, "Don't take any time off to process this or do self-care." It was an old-school way of thinking.

It seemed bizarre to be expected to act like an agent hadn't gotten shot due to serious mistakes. If I had been a manager at the time, I would have said, "Take whatever time off you need!" And I would have ordered mandatory counseling.

✔ Struggling with PTSD

After John's shooting, I kept thinking, That bullet could have struck any agent on the scene! What if it had been me?

Those kinds of thoughts wore on me and kept me up at night. When I was able to get some sleep, I would find myself waking up with hot sweats and cramps. On several occasions, I woke up with my fist within an inch of my wife's face while she slept. One night, Marie actually blocked a punch from me!

I didn't realize it at the time but I was suffering from PTSD.

I would spend hours watching surveillance video footage of the shooting. Over and over again, I reviewed and dissected it, trying to figure out exactly what went wrong and what we could have done differently. As I reviewed the footage, it was clear to me that there were many fundamental operational guidelines not followed that fateful day.

First of all, a UCA should *never* be on scene during a takedown. They are to walk off stage first. Then and only then does the bust team come in and take the bad guys down. That is standard protocol, for obvious reasons.

If we had been properly briefed in advance, the eyes in the sky (the surveillance guys in the hotel) would have been able to stop everyone from proceeding with the arrest until the UCA was safely off scene. Had that happened, the bullet from the supervisor's weapon might have hit the trunk of the car or something other than the UCA.

Secondly, the inexperienced supervisor-driver who inadvertently shot John wasn't switched on. As he was rolling onto the scene to effect the arrest, he was doing too many things at once: The car he was driving was still rolling…he was pulling his weapon out…he was trying to get the car in park…and he was opening the car door with his left hand. With all these things going on at once, it's not surprising that he accidentally discharged his weapon.

Thirdly, the inexperienced supervisor-driver should never have taken it upon himself to effect the arrest in the first place. He was merely assisting on the case, along with some of his agents. Maybe he wanted to play Mr. Big Shot by being the one to effect the arrest. I don't know.

What I do know is this: Just like in the making of a movie, a supervisor needs to pick a role and stick with it. In agency operations, it doesn't work to try to be both the director and the lead actor. Something is bound to go wrong. This case was a classic (and tragic) example of that.

And fourth, the other supervisor—the one who had decided that we didn't need a proper briefing—shared the blame and responsibility for John getting shot. He was not switched on either. Had he stopped and thought about it, he would have realized that it was insane to skip the briefing.

Still, I couldn't shake the feeling that I was partially responsible for John getting shot. I was the one who had suggested going with a live load. Any time we went with a live load, there was more at stake. The bust team was especially hyped up because no one wanted to be responsible for a "loss load" and all the memos to Headquarters that would follow. Losing drugs reflects poorly on the agents involved.

I also looked at my own failure to speak up and insist we have a briefing, and tried to understand my hesitation. I was such a junior agent at that point, I was counting on those above me to do the right thing. My brief stint as a Secret Service Agent had left me with a belief in the layer effect, where if a threat gets through one layer of a security perimeter, someone closer to the protectee would catch it.

It took me months, maybe even years, to come to grips with John's shooting and the mistakes that were made. I was haunted by memories of being at the hospital with John after the shooting, and watching him and his family suffer.

I also struggled to make peace with the way the agency responded, and their failure to discipline both supervisors. As I mentioned, one was sent to a desk job in D.C. The other one stayed in his current position.

I would live with empathy for John and his family, coupled with anger at the agency for failing to take proper operational action with the briefing, and failing to take proper disciplinary action toward the two supervisors responsible.

✔ Putting My Survival Ahead of My Job

John's shooting taught me an invaluable—and indelible!—lesson about listening to one's gut and taking action. From then on, I would always listen to my gut. On the rare occasion when a supervisor insisted I do something that didn't feel right, I would kick the matter up the chain of command.

Months later I was given an unnecessarily dangerous assignment by one of the two inexperienced supervisors on the drug smuggling case (the non-shooter supervisor who decided to skip the briefing).

A shipment of drugs had been confiscated and was being stored in a New York City warehouse. I was put on security detail and ordered to watch the warehouse. I was supposed to make sure no bad guys got wind of the fact that the drugs were there and showed up to steal them. The supervisor assigned me as the only agent posted outside the building watching the shipment, from midnight to 8:00 a.m.

It didn't make any sense to have only one person on the street watching a warehouse full of drugs. It went against all protocol and common sense.

For one thing, everyone knows that it is unsafe to sit in a car by yourself in New York City at night. Secondly, if I was watching a warehouse full of confiscated drugs, and some bad guys showed up with the intention to steal the drugs, I could have ended up in an arrest situation without any backup. Lastly, it was never wise to enter a warehouse full of drugs without another agent to vouch for me. If any of the drugs wound up missing, I could have found myself in a bad position.

So, I said to my supervisor, "You're f**king nuts! What are you doing putting me out on the street alone?"

"What is it, Eric? Is this John shooting really bothering you that much?"

He was damned right it was bothering me. I couldn't believe that he was putting me in harm's way so soon after his poor decision, and that of his fellow supervisor, had led to John becoming paralyzed.

John's words were still ringing in my head. One evening while he was in the hospital receiving treatment after the shooting, we agents were taking turns standing post at his hospital bed. We were there for security purposes and to be of support to his family.

John looked at me and said, "I should have spoken up, Eric, and said I wasn't going to go through with it because we weren't following proper procedures by skipping the operational briefing. Everything was happening so fast and I just got caught up. I felt like I couldn't say no."

"I totally get it," I said. "I should have spoken up and said something myself!"

"Listen," he said, "if you are ever uncomfortable with an operational plan or assignment, don't do it! As you can see, I should have backed out and now I'm paralyzed."

Remembering my friend's admonition to me, I decided to trust my gut. I felt that it was unsafe to be the sole agent watching a drug warehouse. In this case, trusting my gut meant disobeying a direct order.

I did go to New York City, as assigned, but I did not spend the hours between midnight and eight in the morning sitting alone in a car in front of the warehouse full of drugs. Instead, I spent the night in my car in a well-lit, safe location not too far from the warehouse I was supposed to be watching.

I didn't leave the area entirely. That way, in case something went down, I could have claimed that I had just left the warehouse momentarily to use the bathroom or get coffee, and I could have promised to hustle right back over there.

After this, I requested a transfer out of the drug group and into the National Security Group. As I went into future assignments, I always kept John's words fresh in my mind. Learning from what happened to him was not only wise but also a way of making sure something positive came from the tragedy he suffered.

✔ Joining the National Security Group

The New Jersey National Security Group was known throughout the agency as the finest counter-proliferation group in the country. The cases were all about preventing weapons-of-mass-destruction materials from being illegally acquired by foreign hostile nations. The cases centered on Russia, China, Iran, and Iraq, and their efforts to purchase American-made military and dual-use technology.

I was quickly read into our phony New Jersey front company and wired with video and recording devices. And our team was given a Mercedes Benz to share so we could look the part as we wined and dined these foreign buyers and their Stateside representatives.

One day, I was called into my boss's office and handed a letter from a defense contractor.

"Take a look at this and come back to me in a week," he said.

I said to myself, *My first national security case! I am so excited!*

As I read the letter, my excitement faded. The letter alleged that this defense contractor's competitor (Electrodyne Systems Corp. or ESC) was in negotiations with the Taiwanese Government to provide military radar equipment that would not have been allowed for export without certain U.S. Government licenses.

The State Department would not likely have approved the sale of this sensitive military equipment to the Taiwanese government. Taiwan was not a big security threat to the U.S.—but the U.S. Government controls the exportation of all military technologies to *all* other countries. It doesn't matter whether or not the country is deemed to be a state sponsor of terrorism, or a foreign hostile nation. There is no guarantee that a foreign non-hostile nation wouldn't pass along the technology to another country that we *do* deem as a security threat.

This matter seemed to be a simple case of, "Hey! We are law abiding and we play by the rules, but ESC does not, and that's not fair!"

A poison-pen letter was not exactly what I was hoping for when I transferred into the National Security Group.

My boss felt compelled to dot the I and cross the T and put the matter to bed, so he assigned it to the new agent (me), saying, in so many words, "Here you go, kid! Knock yourself out!"

Most seasoned agents would have taken the letter, shredded it, and said to their boss, "Screw you! I'm not wasting my time on this."

As the new guy, I didn't have that leverage. So, I called and arranged a meeting with the president of the defense contractor company. I needed to get more detailed information from him about the who, what, when, where and how. I wanted to find out exactly what the military technology was that ESC was peddling to the Taiwanese Government. And I needed to ascertain whether or not ESC was truly in violation of complicated U.S. export laws.

When I asked the president of the defense contractor company if he knew anyone inside ESC, he said, "As a matter of fact, I do. I have a former employee who is now working there."

"Oh, great! That could prove to be very helpful. Do you think you can get him to the table so we can talk?"

Days later, a meeting was arranged with the president of the defense contractor company and the ESC employee. That meeting lasted four hours, during which I was overwhelmed with information.

It was brought to my attention that this low-level ESC employee had seen wooden crates of Russian hardware entering the facility.

Suddenly, this "Go buy yourself an ice cream, kid," case took on a whole different dimension when the Russian crates got involved.

Over the course of the next couple of years, it would come to light that ESC, a U.S. defense contractor:

- Certified, under penalty of perjury, in signed government military contracts, that they would be manufacturing military goods in the U.S.—a condition of the contracts;
- Signed these contracts knowing fully well that they planned to subcontract the actual manufacturing to former Russian and Ukrainian military facilities;
- Exported the specs, schematics, and technology needed for their Russian and Ukrainian subcontractors to manufacture these U.S. military goods;
- Imported these goods back into the U.S.;
- Falsified U.S. Customs paperwork by listing these Russian and Ukrainian manufactured military goods as goods intended for non-military purposes and usage;
- Painted over country-of-origin markings and passed off these goods as U.S.-made; and
- Charged the U.S. government prices inflated by several multiples over the prices paid to their Russian and Ukrainian subcontractors for the manufacturing of these goods.

✔ Opening Pandora's Box

That night, I wasn't yet sure what violations ESC may have been involved in, but I knew that I had opened Pandora's Box. What had started out as a busy-work assignment given to me as the new kid on the block would end up taking me on a wild, multi-year journey, both professionally and personally.

This case would end up being the very first U.S. Government prosecution over critical military *technology* versus a military commodity, and be featured in many newspapers around the world. It would also bring me before Congress.

Our source was claiming that ESC simply scanned the documents, pressed a button (emailed), and sent documents that showed up in Russia. There was no precedent yet for pressing a button and sending documents electronically over the internet. It was still science fiction at that time.

So, as the old-timer president of the defense contractor was trying to educate me about the phenomenon of being able to export technology via the internet, I couldn't wrap my brain around it. It was unfathomable—something right out of the classic T.V. show, *The Jetsons*.

I was saying, "Wait a minute...ESC is providing a defense service to Russians while in New Jersey? How does that happen?"

I could understand FedEx, U.S. Mail, fax machines, but the ability to email documents was incomprehensible at the time. It was the mid-1990s and the internet wouldn't be ubiquitous yet for a few more years.

It was a real undertaking, trying to convince the government attorney that we had a case. It was a tedious year or two as we tried to establish a case, during which we were dumpster diving (searching through the bad guy's trash) and trying to compile sufficient evidence, all the while giving ourselves a crash course in how the internet worked.

As the case progressed, the prosecutor and I looked at the situation and said, "This stinks but where is the crime?"

We had to tease out the violation. Ultimately, we began to understand the nuances and concluded that we could still argue illegal exportation of a defense service. We reasoned that if it was illegal to export a defense service, under the law it wasn't just the hardware that was being physically exported but also the *technology*—the specs and schematics.

If an item was deemed a controlled commodity under the law, it stood to reason that most if not all of the specs would be deemed controlled as well. And regardless of whether those specs and schematics were sent to the Russians and Ukrainians via the internet or mailed or carried, one way or another that was still exportation.

✔ Facing an Unthinkable Tragedy

One day as I sat down for dinner, Marie suddenly said, "Eric, I want to start a family!"

I almost fell off my chair. Just a few weeks earlier, she had said she wasn't ready and was enjoying working for Continental Airlines and travelling. A few months later she was pregnant and we were ecstatic.

Eddie was at Boston University coaching football when I sent him an ultrasound picture of his future niece or nephew. He wasn't just my twin brother—he was my soulmate. Any time I got big news, good or bad, I wanted to share it with him.

He was thrilled that he was going to be Uncle Eddie.

At 3:00 a.m. in the morning on March 1st, 1994, after a thorough year-long investigation, I was awakened by a phone call from a Customs Inspector who intercepted a crate of Russian components destined for ESC. This was the probable cause I had been waiting for. Now I could get my search warrant.

Later that same day, I was at the U.S. Attorney's Office, finalizing my search warrant on ESC. While putting the finishing touches on my affidavit and getting ready to see a Federal Judge, I received a devastating call I would never forget.

"Call your mom. Your twin brother Eddie died in his sleep," said a senior agent.

I thought, *This guy's got to be busting my chops. I just saw Eddie a few weeks ago!*

So, without hesitation, I said, "F**k you!"

The concept that my healthy twin brother was now dead seemed completely divorced from reality. We had been together only weeks earlier at Giants Stadium in New Jersey when he invited me to be his guest at a Boston University Yankee Conference Football Championship dinner.

Although appearing tired and worn out at that dinner, Eddie or "Chief" was his usual happy-go-lucky self. He did say that he had been ill for a few days but we both chalked it up to a common virus.

My brother was very proud of me and told his players that I was a fed. Then he asked to see my credentials. "Hey, Eric! Let me see your creds. I haven't seen them in a while. Show them to me."

Once he had his hands on my credentials, he started yelling that he was really a Federal Agent and his players better get up against the wall for a pat-down! Then he pretended to frisk the guys. It was a typical Eddie Caron moment.

As we looked down on Giants Stadium during a V.I.P. tour that night, we talked about our dad, and how proud he must have been of us both. Before getting into a van to leave and head back to Boston, he kissed me goodbye, gave me a heartfelt hug and said, "I love you, bro."

Eddie Caron was life, the essence of love and laughter. He would fill up a room with his presence. He loved everyone for who they were and didn't get caught up in trivial fights with siblings.

So, I thought, *This can't be true! Eddie can't be dead!*

I immediately called my mom, praying that it wasn't true.

She answered the phone, crying. "Eddie is gone...he's gone!"

Then I called a best friend of Eddie's and mine, Chris Wheelden.

"Chris," I said, "I'm sorry to tell you this but Eddie died this morning at home in his sleep."

He was shocked, of course.

"Chris, I'm wondering if you would mind going to my mom's house and just being there if she needs anything. It's going to take me a while to get home…"

Without hesitation, Chris called a couple other friends of Eddie's and mine, Chris Horn and Kevin Mello. They all made their way to my mom's house. I could only imagine the scene they walked into, with Mom, Eddie's fiancé, Judy, my sisters, and plenty of Police Officers, all grieving. I will be forever grateful to Chris and our other friends who showed up for our family on that dark day.

I remembered Eddie telling me years earlier that he didn't feel he was long for this earth and knew he would die from a heart attack. In retrospect, my brother lived his life like he was dying because he *was,* and I truly believe he knew it. Maybe we should all live like Eddie. The world would a better place.

I was remembering how Eddie, who had very little money, somehow found a way to have a replica Championship Ivy League ring made for me. He wanted us twins to have twin rings. I would cherish the ring forever as a symbol of the unbreakable bond between us.

I thought about how we had both struggled financially during college. Eddie had little money for food and had to couch-surf during his last two years at college. And I drove a broken-down car that was constantly overheating on the Boston Expressway as I commuted three hours a day (an hour and a half each way), and borrowed money from our sisters to pay for textbooks.

I reflected back on Eddie's football career. After being captain of the football team at his high school, New Bedford High, he went on to Springfield College to study physical education and play college football. Then he landed his first football coaching job as an assistant at Cornell University and then Boston University.

My brother was only twenty-seven when he accomplished a feat that few college or professional coaches could imagine. He won not one but two championship rings, the first at Cornell University (1990 Ivy League Champions) and the second at Boston University (1993 Yankee Conference Champions). That season marked B.U.'s best season in school history, a 12-1 NCAA Division I-AA record.

✔ Sharing the Sad News with Our Loved Ones

After Eddie's death, I was encouraged to go home by the Assistant U.S. Attorney who was helping me draft the search warrant in the ESC case. After a year of hard work, I was determined to see a Federal Judge that day. I knew that both my dad and Eddie would have insisted on it.

The judge told me he was sorry for my loss, granted my warrant, and gave me ten days to execute it.

Once I had the warrant in hand, all I could think about was how was I going to tell Marie that Eddie was gone. She was six months pregnant and attending a community college thirty minutes away.

As I drove, my mind replayed all the great times Eddie and I spent together, whether we were playing sports, attending school, being altar boys, or the millions of other things we did together as twins.

The tears flowed so much while I was driving that it was difficult to see out the windshield and stay focused on the road. Somehow, I made it to the college.

Marie was in an art class. As I peeked in the windows of her class, I saw her laughing and having a good time with her classmates. I stood there watching and knowing I was about to crush this beautiful person who wouldn't kill an ant. Eddie was the brother she never had and he watched over her while I spent months at the Academy.

I finally interrupted the class and said I needed to speak with her. I initially said that Eddie was sick but she could see it was more and persisted with questions.

I finally told her, "Eddie died this morning."

She collapsed in my arms onto the school's hallway floor.

We made our way home and the phone began to ring. My sister Lynn called and so did Eddie's boss, Dan Allen, Head Coach of B.U. Football.

I listened in disbelief as they offered condolences. It was surreal and I was completely at a loss for words.

As Marie and I flew from Newark to Boston, I was still at a loss for words. It wasn't my pain I was feeling but the anticipation of facing the pain of everyone else—my mother, my wife, my five sisters, Eddie's fiancé and friends. I was Eddie's twin, so all eyes would be on me. I had nowhere to hide now and it was all very overwhelming.

I kept asking myself, *Why would an apparently healthy twenty-eight-year-old fall asleep and not wake up?*

We were met at Logan Airport by the same three friends who had earlier shown up at our family home to support my mother. They swept us up and escorted us to Emery Street. It was close to 10:00 p.m. as we took that hour drive home from the airport.

When we arrived, I was met outside by Judy who had discovered my brother's cold, lifeless body upstairs in my parent's home. She told me how much Eddie loved me and how proud he was of me. I could see my mom at the front door, tears rolling down her face as I walked up the front steps. I tried to be strong but to no avail.

Mom collapsed in my arms. All she said was that she tried to save him by doing mouth-to-mouth resuscitation, but he was already gone.

I am still haunted by the vision of my tiny arthritic, cancer-survivor mother trying to save my brother, and then having to watch his lifeless body being carried out in front of her.

✔ Losing My Other Half

I eventually made my way upstairs to the room where Eddie had passed. I sat on the bed and said very little and just reflected on our many wonderful memories. As I've said, my twin loved life and loved making people laugh. Now he was at peace and would be reunited with our dad.

I thought about how, starting around age ten and continuing through our teen years, Eddie and I would dress up as women for Halloween. As I've mentioned, we enjoyed dressing up as sexy, sophisticated businesswomen and we would have a contest to see who had the bigger boobs and hair.

We enjoyed proudly walking in our heels in Halloween parades and trick-or-treating throughout our neighborhood streets, collecting candy. We loved all the laughs we got. And, when my brother was the New Bedford High School Football Captain, he always dressed as a woman for special events because he loved getting laughs from the student body and faculty.

I even witnessed Eddie shave his head when he was seventeen, and then walk into a local Dunkin' Donuts dressed as a woman. My brother was wearing a stuffed bra underneath a lovely dress, along with high heels and a wig. Our cousin Audrey was with him but I stayed outside in her car because I was too embarrassed to go inside.

One of the guys sitting next to him leaned over and said, "You're one ugly bitch!"

To that, Eddie stood up and said, "What did you say?" as he removed his wig.

The whole place erupted with laughter. Eddie Caron deeply believed in the Hindu proverb that states, "True Happiness consists in making others happy."

That first night after Eddie's death, Marie and I slept at Mom's house on the floor in our parlor. Or, should I say, we tried to sleep. I was up all night and could hear my mother crying off and on.

It reminded me of the days and months following Dad's death when Eddie and I often lay awake, listening to our mother sobbing. She usually slept with my dad's photo. Now, on this night, and in the nights to come, she kept Eddie's photo alongside her, as well. I spent that night wondering when I would be the next Caron to die from heart disease. First, it had taken my grandfather, then my father, and now my twin brother.

My anxiety was heightened the very next day by the Medical Examiner who called me to say Eddie apparently died from Hypertrophic Cardiomyopathy, a hereditary heart disease that would have required a heart transplant. He went on to say that I very well may have the same heart disease.

It was tough enough knowing that I was forever a twin-less twin and planning my brother's funeral. Now I wondered if I would live to see my unborn child. I was only twenty-eight and I had already lost my father and my twin brother, my soulmate, to a heart condition.

Now I was asking myself, *Am I next?*

✔ The Circle of Life

On March 2nd, 1994, in New Bedford, after a sleepless night on my mom's living room floor, the sun came up. Sleeping in my childhood room and bed would have been too difficult, thanks to all my fond memories of Eddie. That was the room where we had laughed together, cried and dreamed.

As we prepared for the mass that was being offered that morning for Eddie, I was exhausted. I had barely slept due to my own anguish and the sounds of my mother's cries echoing through the night. Along with a few family members, Mom and I went to church.

Thankfully, I had been able to convince my mother not to have the funeral mass at St. James. I just couldn't handle the added emotional weight of having my brother's funeral take place in a church where I had so many memories. St. James was where Eddie and I were baptized, did our first communion together and were altar boys. I was married there and my brother was my best man. So, we decided on a lovely church in a neighboring town.

Now, we had to attend to all the funeral details. The funeral would be held at Saunders Funeral Home in New Bedford. It had been in business for a hundred years, and they were friends of the family and handled my father's service, as well. To this day, my father's funeral was one of the biggest funerals they had ever handled.

I was accompanied to the funeral home by my mom, my sisters and Judy. Eddie's one and only suit was given to Rick, the funeral director, and the unthinkable task of selecting a casket began. I let the girls pick it out. I knew that Eddie wouldn't have cared two cents about the quality of a casket. Quite frankly, neither did I.

As we all got ready to leave, I felt the need to see Eddie. I couldn't wait any longer. Part of me still couldn't believe he was gone.

I pulled Rick aside and asked, "Is Eddie here?"

"Yes."

"I need to see him now…by myself."

Rick graciously agreed.

I told my family I'd be right back.

My sister Cheryl later told me that she knew where I was going. As I walked downstairs into the basement, the fear of death gripped me.

Rick opened a large walk-in fridge.

I took a deep breath and said under my breath, "Help me, Dad." My head and eyes were down and I sheepishly raised them to see my soulmate on a metal slab. Due to the autopsy, his head had staples from one ear to the other as well as from his chest to his stomach.

Seeing him like that crushed me!

"Oh Eddie...why?" I said, as I cried over him.

After a few minutes, I left, only to return two hours later. I felt the need to go back and see Eddie again. My brother-in-law Glenn, who had just arrived in town, agreed to come with me.

As I reflect back, I'm not sure why I needed to see my brother a second time. Maybe I needed to say to Glenn, "Look! He's actually dead. Can you believe this?"

Much like our dad's funeral service, Eddie's was just as grand. Instead of Police Officers, the steps were lined with B.U. football players and staff.

I jokingly said to the funeral director, "When the Carons go home, we go big!"

Now I had to walk alone, not only escorting my mother up and down the aisle, but also Judy.

I was cursing Eddie out the whole time. I couldn't believe he had left me with this unthinkable task. I wished the roles could have been reversed. I would have gladly taken his place inside that casket.

The eulogies given were beautiful. A priest that knew our family gave the actual eulogy. Then the head coach, Dan Allen, and one of the football captains, Marc Fauci, also shared some remembrances.

Head Coach Allen, a well-respected man, said, "Anyone who knew Ed loved him!"

He went on to describe "the Chief" as a hardworking assistant who always had a smile on his face and enjoyed making others laugh.

Marc Fauci, said, "Ed was a hard worker. He didn't demand respect—he commanded it! And he respected anyone who worked hard."

Eddie would be laid to rest with our father. In his death, my brother was reunited with the man who gave him life.

✔ A Twin-less Twin

Losing Eddie ended my life as I knew it.

Since the moment of our conception, we were together. When he died, I died too. It was no longer "Eddie and I," "Eddie and Eric," or "we." The "we" was broken, physically destroyed. I felt like half a person.

Eddie was the firstborn, physically bigger and louder than me. I was often in his shadow, which I didn't necessarily mind. Now, I was individual.

A shared approach to life is something I was born into as a twin. This is hardwired into me. Unlike my relationship with Marie, my relationship with my twin began before birth. I learned to rely on Eddie in utero and vice versa, and this continued during our lives together. Now, I truly felt like a living, breathing memorial.

On March 7th, 1994, Marie presented me with a card with these words: "Just remember that Eddie is with your dad, and they need each other too." (Remember, Marie's words were coming from a person who lost her younger sister in a motor-vehicle accident just days before Christmas in 1989.)

They were deep meaningful words, and powerful. But I didn't truly understand them at the time. Later, I realized that Eddie longed to be with our dad again.

After all the services, Judy presented me with Eddie's personal belongings discovered in his locker at B.U. Amongst the football clothing was the copy of our baby's ultrasound I had faxed to him a month earlier. I was happy that Eddie had gotten to see his nephew.

My Auntie Barbara, Uncle Pete's wife, presented me with a poem she had personally written, entitled *God's Miracles*:

Two children sat
On a sandy beach
One munched an apple
The other a peach

I wonder why that wave
Wears a little white hat
The child munching the apple
Asked from where he sat

Listen to this shell
Said the child with the peach
It's as if the ocean's roar
Was within arm's reach

I guess it's all miracles
Was the first boy's reply
As he wiped away sand
That had blown in his eye

God must be an artist
The second child said
For look how He's made
The sunset all red

They turned now to look
From one to the other
Each looking into the eyes
Of the other's twin brother

Neither of them thought
Of themselves as odd
Though truly they're miracles
Created by God

Signed: "With love to Eric, Auntie Barbara"

✔ Finishing What I Started

I returned to Newark to execute my warrant with a team of agents. It was difficult to leave my mother so soon after Eddie's death. Then again, work gave me a purpose and distracted me from grief. It also helped keep my mind off my own fear of finding out I'd inherited the same condition that killed my twin.

As I mentioned earlier, this would be the very first Department of Justice prosecution of this specific offense. The internet was a brand-new landscape and we were in virgin territory, which made me worry that the case could go south over prosecutorial timidity.

On government cases, the level of proof is not reasonable doubt—it is *no* doubts. The mere possibility of losing a case at trial (assuming that the defendants don't plead out and the case even makes it to trial) is enough to keep most government attorneys from prosecuting. They actually prefer cases to plead out before they get to trial because that way there is zero chance of losing at trial.

Thankfully, in this case, my fears were unfounded. The case was moving forward.

From time to time, the Assistant U.S. Attorney (AUSA) would mention to me that he thought that the two targets might voluntarily surrender. The AUSA would have preferred it that way—having the bad guys do an arranged voluntary surrender to U.S. Marshals.

I wasn't having it. As far as I was concerned, we had worked hard for years on this case, and I wanted the criminals arrested, like any other international arms smugglers. Having them voluntarily surrender would have been extremely anti-climactic. Not only that, but these criminals had their passports and giving them a heads up about our plans to arrest them could have easily caused them to flee.

I convinced the AUSA that it was unlikely that the ESC bad guys would surrender, and I made him promise that they would be arrested.

He did promise.

I wasn't entirely convinced. After all our hard work, I was leaving nothing to chance. Leading up to the final draft of the arrest warrants, I would often take out my handcuffs and click them to remind him of his promise.

✔ Things are Looking Up

Three months later on June 30th, 1994, Jacob Edmond Caron was born. I believed that Jacob was a gift from God—and Eddie.

God's timing was perfect. Jacob gave me inspiration to live again.

Death and birth…we all move between these two unknowns, trying to understand them both as separate when they are actually the same. With Jacob's birth, I began to understand life. I realized that it didn't start with me and if I do it right, it won't end with me.

The stress of traumatic events, along with the responsibilities that went along with being an agent, a dad and a husband often weighed heavily on me. Thankfully, my dedication to wellness and the joys of family life saved my sanity. Sometimes, I believe they saved my very life.

Because the Medical Examiner wasn't sure of the exact cause of death, I had months earlier consulted with an independent New Jersey pathologist who examined Eddie's heart tissue.

On July 15th, 1994, he brought me into the lab and said, "Look under the microscope. Now look at this medical textbook."

"Wow! The images look exact." I had a piece of Eddie right in front of me.

"You're right," the doctor said. "Your brother clearly died from a virus that attacked his heart. The virus is known as myocarditis. And the good news is that it is not hereditary!"

It was an emotional time. I was learning that I was in no imminent danger of dying from the same heart condition as my twin. I no longer had to worry about falling asleep and never seeing Marie and Jacob again.

As I lived for two-and-a-half years with the nuanced ESC case, I still practiced SEE—trying to eat right, get enough sleep and exercise. I jogged and lifted weights at the gym to alleviate stress. Before bed, I did sit-ups and push-ups, just as Dad had taught us to do when we were kids. I also made an appointment at Mass General Hospital for testing and consultation with a top cardiologist. Thankfully, he determined that my heart was in good condition.

I began praying with Jacob every night, just as my father had done with Eddie and me. I did this not just for my son and my family, but for me as well. Prayer gave me the strength to continue the good fight of prosecuting this case. It would have been very easy for me to give up.

I never got to spend a lot of time with my dad because he worked his ass off. In the limited time I did spend with him, he instilled in us a good work ethic, faith and the importance of honor and duty to family and country. Dad condensed those lessons he needed to teach us into the limited amount of time he had on earth. Now, these things were a part of my DNA.

I think that, like Eddie, our dad may have had a sense that he wouldn't live long. When he was still just a boy, he lost his own dad to a massive heart attack. And in his work as a Police Officer, he saw death all around him all the time. That probably explains why, when he prayed with Eddie and me when we were kids, he taught us that tomorrow is promised to no one.

We knew that every time we lay our heads on the pillow, there was a chance we might not wake up in the morning. I think that this would have created deep anxiety in me if Dad hadn't coupled those lessons with preparation. As I've said, he prepared us for life, and taught us to be little Marines.

I learned so much from my dad—but my stamina and persistence came from my mother. Watching her solider on despite debilitating health challenges taught me so much. Mom never gave up.

✔ Closing the Landmark Case

Two years later, on March 4th, 1996, with Eddie close to my heart, I executed two arrest warrants for the president and vice president of ESC.

I alleged that with the advent of the internet and the fall of the Soviet Union, the bad guys emailed or "exported" military specifications and provided assistance or know-how either electronically, by mail, or by travelling to former Russian and Ukrainian military factories to offshore the production of U.S. military contracts. And I alleged that once the military components were imported into America, the bad guys would paint over any Russian logos and subsequently provide these goods to the U.S. Military as U.S.-made when in fact they were not.

I also alleged that these Russian and Ukrainian components were to be installed in the F-15 Supersonic Fighter Missile System; the firing mechanism used on U.S. Navy ships to control both the ship's guns and surface-to-air missile; an Advance Medium Range Air-to-Air Missile Program; and an airborne surveillance project, code name "Gusty Badger," just to name a few contracts.

The case was widely covered by the news media throughout the world. When the case broke, it was like, *Wow, I've actually pulled this off!* It was featured on CNN, and in both The Washington Post and The New York Times.

Less than a year later, the defendants copped a plea, and served reduced sentences of only about one year each. Additionally, the corporation paid a million-dollar penalty.

On May 15th, 1996, I appeared before the Permanent Subcommittee on Investigations, U.S. Congress, for a hearing on Russian Organized Crime in the United States. Marie and little Jacob were right by my side. This was a proud moment not just for me but for the entire Caron family. Now, I felt Eddie on one shoulder and my dad on the other.

The senators' level of interest and concern was appreciated. They openly discussed the grave harm to our national security that ESC could have caused, and thanked my agency for our efforts. The fact that a U.S. defense contractor was exporting military contracts, some classified, most not, to Russia without the U.S. government's knowledge, and selling them as U.S.-made when they were not, presented a clear and present danger.

During the hearing, a discussion ensued related to the fact that the confidence of our military to defend this country rests largely on its ability to operate sophisticated, high-tech systems with the confidence that they meet specifications, safe from sabotage and free from any foreign government's countermeasures.

On June 29th, 1996, I was blessed with the birth of another son, Tyler (Ty) Joseph Caron. Ty's outgoing, lighthearted personality would turn out to be a lot like his uncle Eddie's while Jacob's (Jake's) personality is much more reserved, like mine. In fact, Eddie used to tease me about my reserved, conservative personality saying, "Eric, for God's sake, take your skirt off and lighten up!"

God had given me an Eddie and Eric and I was thrilled. I imagined that my dad must have felt much the same way when he was told he had twin boys.

Throughout my sons' childhood and adolescence, I would carry on the traditions my father had passed down to my brother and me. I prayed with my boys before bedtime, and stressed to them the importance of SEE. I taught them that eating right, sleeping enough, and exercising moderately were the three essential things they should do each and every day. Eat. Sleep. Exercise. I would simply hold up three fingers and they would both instantly say "SEE." It was a simple mantra but effective to this day.

✔ Meeting the Press

Years later, when I was in D.C., I made myself available for in-depth interviews with the press. And on September 15th, 1998, The Washington Post ran a feature story on the smuggling case entitled, "Catching a Pentagon Supplier Smuggling."

The story described in detail how I initiated and investigated this case, including flying to the Naval Research Laboratory (NRL) in Washington, D.C. to examine suspect military amplifiers. It stated that after removing the ESC label, and burning off the paint, Ukrainian markings/logos were exposed. And it mentioned that months of "dumpster diving" at ESC had produced various business documents, including Ukrainian documents with the same logos discovered at NRL.

In addition, on October 25th, 1998, <u>The New Bedford Standard Times</u> would run a feature story on me, the case, and my extended family, entitled *Quiet Heroism*. The feature discussed how I overcame adversity, and stated that I "drew fortitude from...family, faith, and native city."

Ironically, nearly ten years later, this same newspaper and its reporters would unknowingly demonize me, describing how I and other agents conducted a raid like German S.S. Gestapo Officers. They would not realize that they were vilifying the very same agent they had put on the cover earlier with a caption to the effect that this hometown boy had made good and pulled off an amazing national security operation.

✔ Investigating Another Technology Transfer

In September of 1997, I was promoted to Internal Affairs, United States Custom Service, (IA) Headquarters in Washington, D.C. Although grateful for the promotion, I had no desire to make this a long-term assignment. Investigating fellow Special Agents just wasn't my passion.

Thankfully, within the year, a senior manager asked if I would be interested in a six-month temporary duty assignment (TDY) to our Washington D.C. field office to assist on a case relating to Chinese acquisition of U.S. military technology for their missile program. Since I had the first successful prosecution of this type of case, he thought I might add value to the investigation.

I immediately said yes, hoping that the TDY would be permanent.

The criminal case involved the high-profile defense contractors Hughes and Loral Space Systems, but quickly became focused primarily on Hughes. A CIA Analyst and others alleged that Hughes and Loral Space had engaged in unauthorized sharing or transferring of sensitive military and dual-use missile technology to China.

This information was given to several congressional committees, and an investigation ensued over whether technology or information was transferred to the People's Republic of China that may have contributed to the enhancement of nuclear-armed intercontinental ballistic missiles or to the manufacture of weapons of mass destruction.

Earlier that same year, investigations were kicked off with Senate hearings on China's influence in America's 1996 presidential and congressional elections. Simultaneously, the Department of Justice (DOJ) was conducting their own criminal investigations.

The CIA Analyst was not able to recall the names of the Hughes personnel who assisted the Chinese government during a post-accident missile failure investigation. So, one of these committees asked the CIA to retrieve the information from its files.

The agency complied—but they simultaneously alerted the targets (Hughes employees) to the fact that they were targets of an investigation and might be questioned. The CIA even went so far as to provide the targets with the name of the CIA Analyst making the allegation of illegal technology transfer, and gave them a complete roadmap of the investigation, including lines of potential questions.

They did all this without the prior knowledge of the investigating committees or the DOJ. And they did so *while assisting* the DOJ in their investigations. That's right—on the one hand, they were going through the motions of assisting in the investigation, and on the other hand, they were feeding information to the targets of the investigation.

The CIA back-doored us as well by secretly telling the targets about our investigations. It would later come to light in newspaper articles that the CIA's reason for double-crossing everyone was the preservation of their admitted long-standing covert relationship with Hughes and Loral.

So, what began as a criminal case against Hughes and Loral now splintered into an obstruction of justice case against the CIA, and the two cases were walled off from each other. After a few months of assisting the case agents at the DOJ with their criminal investigation of Hughes and Loral, I was asked to lead this investigation of the CIA. I happily agreed since it kept me out of Headquarters and Internal Affairs.

✔ Investigating the CIA

I spent approximately the next six months at CIA Headquarters (Langley) reviewing documents and working alongside investigators from the CIA's Internal Affairs branch, which is known as the Office of Inspector General. (Then there are two congressional oversight committees who also keep an eye on the CIA and make sure they are playing by the rules.)

I and other agents interviewed dozens of CIA employees during that time. Meanwhile, the Department of Justice did something that had never been done before: they issued a Grand Jury Subpoena to the CIA for records and compelled employees, including the General Counsel, to testify under oath before a Grand Jury in Washington, D.C.

The experience really opened my eyes to the world of politics, and the on-goings at Langley and National Resources (NR)—the domestic division of the CIA. It seemed to me that the higher-ups at the CIA believed that they were above the law, and that the ends justified the means. They had a reputation as an arrogant agency that did whatever the hell it wanted to do, and couldn't seem to get out of its own way.

As an agent, I had of course heard stories about the lengths the CIA would go to in order to accomplish their ends. One alarming story related to a former DEA Agent and a Federal Prosecutor who had their conversations eavesdropped on by the CIA while serving overseas. After a fifteen-year legal battle, they won a three-million-dollar civil lawsuit against the CIA.

I was worried that the CIA might have been listening to *my* conversations. I was very transparent about my feelings toward them. I didn't like them much and didn't trust them as far as I could throw them—and they knew it.

As we moved our way, inch by inch, to the very top of the agency, I was concerned that they would feel more and more threatened. I began feeling nervous about my safety. So, I made sure I was always switched on while working on this case. I even checked the underside of my car for explosives on a daily basis.

I spent about a month conducting frustrating interviews of CIA officials from their General Counsel's Office (GCO), Congressional Affairs, and NR, and figured out that they all seemed to be speaking from the same script. All had little to offer as to who ultimately made the decision to notify the targets of the ongoing DOJ/Grand Jury investigation.

On a humid summer day, I scheduled an interview with an attorney from the CIA's General Counsel Office. I harbored little hope that the interview with this witness would be fruitful, given the disappointing interviews I'd already conducted with numerous witnesses. In fact, I was so convinced it was a waste of time, I went to the interview by myself without another agent or the Assistant United States Attorney.

As it turned out, I was pleasantly surprised.

The witness had specific recollection of a pivotal meeting in which an individual from the CIA entered a conference room, filled with General Counsel Office staff and others from Langley who had been waiting for this individual's arrival for the meeting to proceed. The Hughes/Loral investigation was on the agenda for the meeting.

During discussions about the investigation, the CIA recommended that Hughes and Loral give their employees a heads up about these ongoing DOJ/Grand Jury investigations.

My witness respectfully said, "Wait a minute...this is an ongoing DOJ/Grand Jury investigation and it would be really inappropriate to give the targets a heads up!"

In reply, the individual from the CIA said, "I don't care about the DOJ case! We're CIA. We don't take orders from DOJ. Make the notification!"

"I went along to get along," said my witness, "and said to myself, 'Well, I guess I'm in the big leagues now! These seem to be the big dogs on the block.'"

When all was said and done, the ever-so-timid souls at the DOJ stated the party line: after careful assessment of the facts, there was little likelihood of prevailing at trial. The DOJ declined to prosecute any Hughes officials for illegally providing sensitive U.S. technology to China; and also declined to prosecute any CIA officials for obstructing justice related to this investigation. Multimillion-dollar fines were issued to Hughes and Loral, and the CIA was essentially reprimanded with a slap on the wrist.

I figured that the prosecutorial timidity related to several factors, including the close intelligence ties between the agency and defense contractors in general; the multi-million-dollar campaign donations by Hughes and Loral; and the appointment by then President Clinton of the Hughes president to head the U.S. Government's export counsel. I figured that the combination of these compelling factors trumped any criminal wrongdoing.

On December 5th, 1998 The Washington Post published an article entitled "CIA Role in Satellite Case Spurs Probe" in which it states: "High-ranking CIA officials, including the agency's general counsel, have agreed to testify next week before a federal grand jury in Washington about information provided earlier this year to Hughes, which has supplied the CIA with satellites and sophisticated communications equipment for decades…A CIA spokesman said the agency is fully cooperating in the obstruction probe. Another CIA official, speaking on background, acknowledged that the agency may have erred in providing certain information to Hughes…"

Then, in a December 31st, 1998 Wall Street Journal article, it was reported that a bipartisan congressional committee representing the American people spent many months investigating the alleged technology transfers to China by Hughes and Loral and other U.S. companies, and determined that U.S. national security was indeed harmed.

I thought to myself, *Congress claims U.S. national security was harmed and DOJ fails to prosecute anyone? Go figure! Are we all working for the same government and on the same team? Sometimes I'm really not so sure!*

Former President and founding father John Adams instinctively understood the dirty politics of the day and believed that all people are fallible. And he knew that people in positions of power would help their friends and punish their enemies. He sought to establish a government of laws and not of men, enshrining in the 1780 Constitution of the

Commonwealth of Massachusetts these words: "For as in absolute governments the King is law, so in free countries the law ought to be king; and there ought to be no other..."

Like John Adams, I too believe that no man (or institution) should be above the law. So, this outcome was disheartening and disappointing, to say the least.

✔ Investigating the Russians, Take Two

After so many months away from Internal Affairs while assigned to the Hughes-Loral/CIA investigation, IA permanently released me to the Washington D.C. field office for U.S. Customs.

In January of 1999, I was contacted by the same Confidential Informant who had initiated the ESC case. He liked and trusted me and we had developed a good rapport on the ESC case. The CI told me that he was being aggressively pursued by a subject named Mr. Batko who was attempting to acquire for Russia some military radar equipment designed for the U.S.-made F-15J fighter jet. I quickly learned that the J stood for Japanese.

Initially, it was unclear as to why the Russians wanted this technology. I later learned that the Russians supplied billions of dollars' worth of military equipment, including avionics, to the Chinese government. (I figured China might have wanted information on Japanese military equipment because of the thousands of years they had spent at war with Japan.)

A September 11th, 1999 article in The Washington Post entitled "Arms Smuggling Bid Charged" stated: "...Mike Turner, the Customs Service's director of strategic investigations, called the scheme to acquire the avionics 'one of the classic methods used by foreign governments to acquire sensitive military technology either for its direct use or so that it can be reverse engineered'..."

My source agreed to assist Mr. Batko, referring him to his "representative" outside Washington, D.C., who was actually a UCA.

After months of telephone and face-to-face (what we called "grip and grin") meetings, we learned a surprising fact about the people behind the Russian company. They turned out to be the same tech guys responsible for placing hundreds of listening devices throughout the structural shell of the U.S. Embassy in Moscow, using steel beams which served as antennas emitting signals to the KGB. This had resulted in a situation where the entire embassy had to be redesigned.

Mr. Batko paid the UCA one hundred thousand dollars as a down payment, and subsequently asked if the agent would fly to Chicago to meet a representative of the end-user to discuss the transfer of the radar to Russia. The representative was a man named Dr. Press, the former Dean of Moscow State Engineering.

Based on the most recent recordings with the UCA and Mr. Batko, I didn't get a good feeling. Batko was acting cagey and nervous as if he suspected the UCA. I knew that if the UCA wasn't tuned into the fact that Mr. Batko might be tuned into *him*, the whole thing could go south and turn dangerous very quickly.

In preparing for this meeting to be held in the Red Carpet Lounge at O'Hare International Airport, I told the UCA to wear a beeper, which was supposed to function as a beeper, recorder, and transmitter. Unfortunately, as fate would have it, the beeper wasn't working. I requested another beeper but the FBI didn't have a functioning one to give us either. So, we went with a basic recording device.

I was very concerned about having the UCA go forward with the meeting. I knew that by placing the device in his briefcase with the wires run up the sides, the UCA ran the risk of the targets easily discovering it if they became suspicious. If the beeper device had been working, it would have been placed on the UCA's body instead of inside his briefcase and been much easier to hide.

I called him several times in advance of the scheduled meeting to express my concerns.

"Don't worry," he said, trying to reassure me, "I'm all set and ready to go."

"But, without the ability to transmit, you'll be flying solo!" I said.

"Don't worry. All good here."

✔ Avoiding Catastrophe

I made one more call to the UCA the day prior to travel. When we talked, he sounded confident and put my mind at ease. (The UCA always has the final say in an undercover operation, as they have the most to lose.)

As the UCA and the D.C. cover team landed in Chicago, our local agents met us. "We already have Batko under surveillance," they explained, "and he is with another man, presumably Dr. Press."

With the UCA and the cover team in place, the UCA made contact with Mr. Batko who stated that he was in The Red Carpet Lounge, the agreed-upon location.

The bad guys entered and greeted the UCA. Then, speaking a foreign language a translator later confirmed was Russian, Dr. Press told Mr. Batko that he wanted to move to another table. It happened to be closer to one of the agents who had a covert camera recording the meeting. This was a lucky coincidence.

After hours of negotiating, it was agreed that monies would be paid offshore and the radar equipment hand-delivered to a person outside Washington, D.C.

The UCA shook hands with the bad guys and walked over to the customer service center. As he was standing in line to make his flight arrangements back to D.C., Mr. Batko approached him.

"Dr. Press wants me to look inside your bag," said Batko. "He thinks you're wired!"

The agent extracted himself from the conversation by getting angry and saying, "F**k you! If you don't trust me...I don't trust you! The deal is off!"

As we all travelled back to D.C., we were careful to have no contact with the UCA. As I mentioned, the device he was carrying could only record, not transmit. So, we had no ears on him.

The UCA was, however, able to make quick covert contact with one of our agents as they passed each other entering or exiting a bathroom in the lounge where the meeting was held.

"We need to get out of here! Let's roll. They're onto us!" the UCA said.

"We're on it," said the other agent, who then put it out over his radio (which *was* functioning) that we were "wheels up."

Since we had no way of knowing who might have been following the UCA, we did keep constant eyes on him, with multiple guys watching him on the plane. Some were dressed in business casual style and some were dressed as blue-collar workers.

When we landed, we all regrouped back at the office for a debriefing. The UCA was understandably distraught and concerned for his safety. While traveling home, he had been unable to go outside his role to contact us. And even though we had eyes on him everywhere he went, we couldn't approach him because we would have compromised his safety.

Based on all the evidence, we were able to get an arrest warrant for Mr. Batko and Dr. Press and a search warrant for Mr. Batko's home-based business.

I got to bed after midnight and was up and out of the house by 5:00 a.m. It was time to travel back to Chicago to execute these warrants with the help of our local agents.

Finding Mr. Batko was easy but we had no identifiers on Dr. Press. All we had was a name. After arresting Batko, I was able to squeeze just enough information out of him on Dr. Press before he lawyered up.

At approximately 2:00 a.m., we found Dr. Press sleeping at another Russian's home in suburban Chicago.

I thought, *Man, where have you been all my life? I've been looking for you for the last five hours!*

✔ Understanding the Failure to Prosecute

My feeling of exhilaration was snuffed out when, weeks later, the U.S. Attorney's offices in both Virginia and Illinois got cold feet. They declined to prosecute because they had determined that successful prosecution was doubtful. The government attorneys said that they felt that the charge of attempted illegal exportation of a munitions-list article constituted what they called a dry conspiracy.

Since the bad guys had exposed our UCA before he could meet with their representative and hand off the commodity, the bad guys' rep never had the opportunity to attempt to flee the U.S. with it. By definition, that meant that the bad guys never attempted to illegally export the military hardware.

All we had was a one-hundred-thousand-dollar down payment and "dirty talk"—the bad guys and the UCA agreeing on the amount of money still due and payable, and the method of exportation. Unfortunately, the U.S. Attorney's office considered this to be insufficient basis for prosecution.

Had everything gone as planned, the UCA would have met with the representative for the bad guys and given him an item that was dressed up to look like the commodity. Then, once the rep had boarded the plane—creating the basis for prosecution on attempted illegal exportation grounds—we would have boarded the plane and arrested him.

The U.S. Attorney's office was also discouraged by the fact that neither Batko nor Press had prior arrest records.

Nobody likes to lose a case at trial. This is especially true of government attorneys who usually insist on taking only slam-dunk cases to trial. But even some of those cases don't make it to trial. There are several factors behind this:

- the attitude of most government attorneys is, the more positive marks on their record, the better;
- many of them are looking to the next chapter of their lives, which might include a judgeship or a job that requires an especially high wins-to-losses case ratio;
- there is often prosecutorial discretion in these government cases involving white-collar criminals, which means that they *can* decline to prosecute if they so choose;

- government attorneys might be intimidated by Ivy League attorneys representing the target company. Plenty of those attorneys are former Federal Prosecutors themselves and know all of the ins and outs of the Department of Justice; and government attorneys prefer to prosecute low-hanging fruit (meaning, targets without high-stake political entanglements).

When government attorneys want to get out of prosecuting a seemingly open-and-shut case, they often give their standard excuse: "We need more evidence to succeed at trial. If you can't get more evidence, sorry but there will be no prosecution."

It is often more complex than we are led to believe. A recent article in The Washington Post was a great illustration of this. The article, dated December 17th, 2017, was titled, "A Blockbuster Opioid Case, Hijacked."

The article dealt with a major pharmaceutical company that had been warned to stop certain actions because they were in violation of the law. The pharmaceutical company continued in their reckless actions—providing pharmacies, distributors and questionable locations with way too many opioid medications.

The DEA (the investigating agency) stated that the government attorneys turned a blind eye to the pharmaceutical company's illegal actions, effectively hijacking what should have been an open-and-shut, blockbuster opioid case. Instead of prosecuting the case, the government attorneys gave the pharmaceutical company a slap on the wrist, and that was the end of that.

Of course, the DEA's response to this was: "But, we've given you the case on a silver platter! What do you mean you're not going to prosecute?"

The pharmaceutical company in this case was a Fortune 500 company that donated millions of dollars to various political campaigns. It is not hard to imagine the pharmaceutical company calling in a favor from the DOJ, whether directly or through a third party.

Later in my career, when I was working in Congressional Affairs, I would see congressional staffers acting on behalf of their constituents all the time. I heard conversations where a congressional staffer would reach out to a government attorney and say, "My constituent Mr. X, who runs this company, briefed us on this case and he feels he's being unjustifiably hassled here."

Nothing chills a prosecutor more than a call from congressional staffers or the White House, saying, "What is the status of this case? And why was this investigation started?"

During my years as a Special Agent, I often asked myself, *If the mere thought of losing at trial is so untenable to someone, why would they become a Federal Prosecutor in the first place?*

To me, it seems as ludicrous as a young man going through the Police Academy, becoming a Police Officer and then turning around and saying, "Wait a minute, here...I don't want to actually arrest anyone! I just like wearing the uniform."

Once again, I was reminded of John Adams words, and wished that everyone abided by them and no one was treated as above the law.

✔ Handling Disappointment

It is hard to even put into words what a Federal Law Enforcement Agent goes through when government attorneys decline to prosecute after the agent has worked long and hard on a case, often immersing themselves and making sacrifices in their personal lives for years on end. The frustration and crushing disappointment can be too much to handle. It can lead some agents to depression, drug/alcohol abuse, and sadly, even suicide. (More on that later.)

Even when agents don't try to manage their frustration and disappointment with excessive alcohol/drug use, and even when they don't fall into suicidal depression, they can find themselves migrating over to the dark side.

They might say to themselves, *Well, if these criminals whose actions negatively affect countless numbers of people aren't even prosecuted, what's the point of what I do for a living? If the system is totally broken and evil is going to win out over good, I might as well get in on the action.*

I had invested a great deal of time on the Batko case, working my ass off, sacrificing myself and my family. I felt—as I so often did when working on a case—like I was doing the Lord's work and believed that good would prevail in the end. So, it was worth all the family dinners and birthdays I missed while immersing myself in the case.

Then, when the Assistant U.S. Attorney said, "Nice job, but we're not going to prosecute because we view this as a dry conspiracy," I could have let it put a hole in my stomach. After all, we had just arrested two obvious criminals who had paid the UCA one hundred thousand dollars for the illegal acquisition of military equipment. And I knew for a fact that the bad guys we had busted were guilty.

I decided that my best bet was just to move on and start another chapter of my career. So, I said in effect, "Fine. I guess I'll take my ball and go home…and start work on another case."

Thank goodness, I was a seasoned, mature agent by this point in my career and I had the equilibrium to surrender and move on. Perhaps the sudden-death loss of beloved family members had taught me the art of letting go.

At times like these, I also prayed The Serenity Prayer: "God grant me the serenity to accept the things I cannot change; courage to change the things I can; and wisdom to know the difference."

1955 - Korean War - Dad (Right) serving his country in Japan,
Island of Iwo Jima. Mt Suribachi in foreground

1955 - Dad (Center) - Iwo Jima, Japan ready for patrol

1962 - New Bedford Police Department - Dad (left) with his younger brother Pete

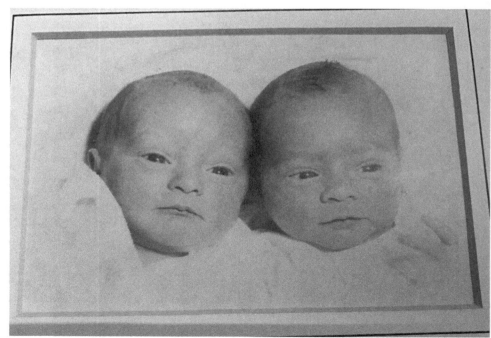

July 24, 1965 - First baby photo with my twin Eddie (left)

June 1966 - Dad Featured in a Father's Day story in the New Bedford Standard Times -
Sister Michelle not born yet

Eddie & I (on left) at 3 years old proudly displaying our Red Sox Jackets

Eddie and I (on left) Sunday Best - with shoes shined.

The Caron's Always Dressed to Impress - "Creative designs by mom & Nana Bolger"

Dad and his "Young Marines"...So Proud

The Caron's Easter Sunday Best

The Caron Family with Boston Celtics Legend Joe Joe White - 1977

The Caron Family with Mayor Markey (Uncle Jack) of New Bedford, Ma - 1974

The author and Eddie playing in our bedroom - American flag can be seen hanging near the bunk beds where we prayed each night with Dad

The Caron Alter boys (Eddie on left)

New Bedford Bronco League Allstars with Coach Caron and his boys. Author on left.

Eddie as "Edith" Senior Year @ New Bedford High School

Opposing Teams - Friendly competition- New Bedford High School vs. New Bedford Voc-Tech - Freshman Year. Author in Green Jersey.

Sgt Caron Leading The Charge - First through the door to apprehend a felon

Sgt Caron pictured with one of his officer's receiving "New Bedford PD Officer of The Year" - Responsible for breaking up an arm robbery in progress @ a local pharmacy.

1984 - New Bedford Voc-Tech High School Graduation - Author with Mom

1982 - Picking Up The Torch - Author (on Rt) and Eddie Accompanying Mayor Markey (Uncle Jack) to his Swearing In Ceremony.

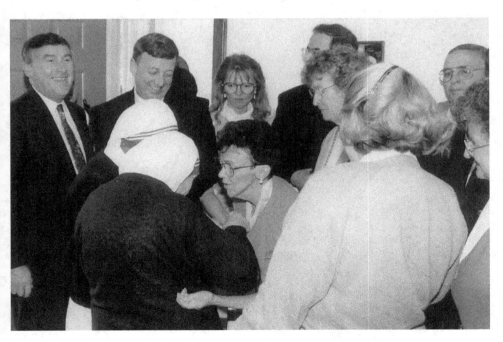

June 14, 1995 - Mom meeting Mother Teresa in New Bedford, Ma - Notice her crippling hand.

Coach Caron (Eddie) with his Fiancee Judy after a Cornell Football Game. Proudly wearing his previous year championship ring

1984 Caron Family Photo for Mom

1990 -Coach Caron (Eddie) with Ivy League Champion Trophy - Cornell University

1993 - Coach Caron (Eddie) with Yankee Conference Trophy & Author holding "Lambert Trophy" This photo is the last one ever of Eddie & I together...he died a few days later.

1986 - Author Wareham Police Department - Summer Police Officer

Author with sons Jacob (left) & Tyler learning the SEE philosophy early.

Author Family Photo

Author with Patrick J. Buchanan during Presidential Campaign

Author with sons Tyler (left) & Jacob

2011 - Author with Secretary General of INTERPOL - Ronald Noble - Dubai, UAE -
Operation Pink Panther

Sept 1989 - Graduation Day from Basic Agent School -Federal Law Enforcement Training Academy with mom

2011 - Dubai Diplomatic Meeting - Author with U.S. Consul General & Director General of Dubai Customs.

2010 - Author providing national security training to Dubai Customs & Police Officials

December 31, 2015 - The Address Downtown New Year's Eve Fire -Dubai - Author lived on the 21st floor After escaping took this photo

Author's bedroom after the Dubai New Year's Eve Fire

December 2010 - Author leading an Anti Money Laundering Training Seminar
in Kabul, Afghanistan - training site was subsequently attacked
by terrorists and several people were killed.

March 6, 2007 - Author (like Father...like son) seen arresting/escorting a Michael Bianco Manager into a Gov't Agent Vehicle - blocks from his childhood home.

Sept 2017 - Author pictured with his class @ The Massachusetts Maritime Academy

IN LOVING MEMORY

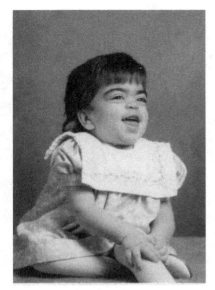

Jennifer McCann

Andrew McCann

The Caron Grave Stone

✔ Taking Time to Dance

I had just been promoted back into the National Security Division (NSD). I viewed Headquarters as a religious retreat—a comparatively peaceful assignment. I was ready to get off the streets for a while, and welcomed the change.

I had applied for a coveted position in the NSD before the AUSA declined to prosecute on the Batko case. I won the position based upon our arrest of Batko and Press, the seizure of one hundred thousand dollars, and the initially great press on the front page of papers like The Washington Post.

In September of 1999, I reported to Headquarters and was assigned to the NSD as a National Program Manager for terrorism. As the new agent, I was responsible for putting together a national training conference in Washington, D.C. for all field agents involved in preventing countries of concern and countries considered state sponsors of terrorism from acquiring WMD materials.

A poster that I had developed with input and approval was entitled *Law Enforcement Solutions for National Security*, and it featured a photo of Osama bin Laden front and center. I still have this poster as a reminder to never forget.

A family moment occurred after arriving back in D.C. that would always stay with me and sweeten the tough times. Jake was six years old at the time and Ty was four. Each evening after dinner, baths, bedtime reading, and prayers, I would hold them both in my arms and slow dance to my favorite R&B love songs. I would then put the boys to bed with a local D.C. classical music station playing ever so softly. (I read articles from time to time that stated that classical music was good for the development of children's brains.)

Well, one early morning at 3:00, after a long day at Headquarters, I was in bed asleep when I heard the boys yelling, "Daddy, Daddy your song is on! Come dance!"

Initially, I thought I was dreaming. *Dance?* I thought. *To classical music? We never dance to classical music.*

I lay there, hoping that after a few seconds they would fall back to sleep, but no such luck. I heard the calls to dance get louder. I stumbled over to the boys' room and opened their door.

There they were, both standing up, crying, with arms reaching out for me.

I immediately swooped them both up and we danced to *Forevermore (I'll be The One)* by James Ingram. The song's lyrics are beautiful: "Before we go to sleep tonight, we'll say our prayers, I'll hold you tight, and kiss away the fears you hold inside you..."

Evidently, the classical station turned overnight into soft R&B music. So, at least once or twice a week for nearly a year, I would dance with both my boys in the early morning hours to one of our favorite R&B love songs.

And you know what? I loved every minute of it, even though it meant that I would be sleep deprived for work that day. This was the kind of unconditional love I learned from my dad.

Funny enough, until the boys were between the ages of seven and ten, they thought their dad was a garbage man. I told them that for their own protection. I felt that the fewer people who knew what I actually did for a living, the better.

One day, when a reporter asked me for a photo of the kids and me, I refused. The kids were present when the reporter made this request and they were upset when I said no. They were too young to understand that my security concerns were well founded. After all, I had helped put many bad guys behind bars, from arms smugglers to international drug cartel members. The threat of retaliation was very real and always a concern for me.

✔ Suffering More Heartbreak

On January 13th, 2000, my sister Lynn called to tell me that our dad's brother, Uncle Pete, was driving his van when he had an apparent heart attack and died. There were those two dreaded words again: heart attack. Uncle Pete was sixty-three years old and was a father figure to me. I was heartbroken over his death. At his funeral services, I was once again reminded of the fragility of life.

Then, in early June of that same year, I received word from my sister Cheryl that our mother was fighting pneumonia. I spoke with Mom and, although she was weak, her spirits were good. When I shared a few details about my current position at work, she enjoyed listening and told me how proud she was of me.

Days later, I received word that she had been transferred to Mass General Hospital. I immediately got on a plane and met my brother-in-law John in Providence, and we drove together to Mass General. As I entered the ward, it suddenly occurred to me that my dad had died there. I wondered if my mom would die there too.

John did his best to prepare me for what I was about to see when I walked into my mother's hospital room—but nothing could have fully prepared me for seeing my mother attached to, and surrounded by, medical equipment. She was already on a ventilator and unconscious.

After several days in Boston, taking turns with my sisters sleeping on the hospital waiting-room floor, I returned to D.C. I needed to be there to manage a counter-proliferation case. My wife and young sons needed me, as well.

Within a week, a team of doctors asked our family for permission to conduct a "routine examination" of Mom's brain activity. I was already back in D.C. by then.

Days later, I returned to Mass General with Marie and the kids. I had just arrived back in Boston when the doctor called me, nearly in tears, to apologize.

Apparently, during the so-called routine test, the anesthesiologist failed to properly ventilate my mother. As a result, she was without oxygen for nearly eight minutes. Now, if she were to live, she would be a vegetable.

✔ Sending Mom Home to Dad

E ven though our family understood that Mom would never regain normal brain function, it was excruciating to make the decision to turn off the ventilator.

After having spent several days at Mass General, Marie and I drove the eight hours back to D.C. But the minute we walked into the house, the phone was ringing. It was my sister Cheryl. All of my sisters were gathered around Mom's hospital bed and they had jointly decided it was best to turn off the machine.

I told Cheryl that I was on board with my sisters' decision. I also told her that Marie and the kids and I would get some sleep and then return to Boston for funeral and burial arrangements.

Cheryl placed the phone to my mother's ear for me to say goodbye one last time. With the sounds of my sisters crying in the background, and the strains of *Fly Me to The Moon*, Mom's favorite Frank Sinatra song which my sisters were playing for her on a boombox, I said goodbye to my mother.

"Goodbye, Mom, I love you. Thank you for being a great mom. And please say hello to Dad and Eddie for me."

As I was saying goodbye, the Frank Sinatra song ended and my sisters played a Phil Collins song for Mom. The song was *You'll Be in My Heart*.

The lyrics to the song begin like this:

Come stop your crying
It will be all right
Just take my hand
And hold it tight

I will protect you
From all around you
I will be here
Don't you cry...

Cause you'll be in my heart
Yes, you'll be in my heart
From this day on
Now and forever more

You'll be in my heart
No matter what they say
You'll be here in my heart
Always...

The song ends with these words: *Just look over your shoulder, just look over your shoulder, just look over your shoulder, I'll be there...Always.*

When I look over my shoulder, I often see a butterfly.

My sisters stayed gathered around our mother's hospital bed, holding her hands. And then the medical staff shut off all the machines sustaining my mother's life. At sixty-two years old, Mom was gone.

✔ Appreciating My Mother's Sacrifices

My mother was born on March 8th, 1938, and was one of eight children. Her family lived in a two-bedroom apartment in Fall River, Massachusetts, a blue-collar textile city. Mom's mother was a seamstress, and her father was a painter who was a bookie on the side to earn extra money to feed the family.

With barely enough money to heat their small apartment, the older kids went out and collected coal that had fallen off the railroad cars, and brought it home for heat. Then they would huddle together in their beds and try to stay warm.

Mom was only nineteen when she got diagnosed with crippling rheumatoid arthritis. The girl who was one of eight children went on to have seven children of her own.

During her lifetime, Mom endured decades of pain from the arthritis in her hands. It got so bad that she had all of her knuckles replaced and spent months dealing with physical therapy. As the years went by, the amount of medication (pills and "gold shots") Mom received to help alleviate pain and discomfort from the arthritis increased too.

At one point, the dreadful disease moved to Mom's neck. Stretching her neck and back brought her relief, so a makeshift traction system was set up. Here's how it worked. Mom would sit in a chair with her back against a door and a harness around her neck. A pulley system went over the door, balanced by a sandbag filled with sand I had collected from the beach. This was truly a scene from medieval times.

My siblings and I would take turns setting up this contraption. Then one of us would slowly ease down the bag of sand to help stretch Mom's neck and back. I lived with fears and nightmares over the thought of inadvertently decapitating my own mother as I lowered the sandbag, and I was haunted by her cries of pain during these makeshift traction sessions.

Although Mom endured a lifetime of pain, it didn't stop her from cooking, baking and making clothes for all of us kids. She actually taught cake decorating to seventh and eighth graders at St. James School. One student even attributes her degree in Pastry Arts to my mother.

Despite the crippling pain that she lived with, Mom volunteered each Sunday to give the holy eucharist. The flatness of the eucharistic wafer made it difficult for her to grab with her arthritic fingers and it often took her several attempts, as people stood waiting in line at her station for the holy bread.

When Mom finally got a grip on the wafer, she would raise her crippled hand, and say, "The body of Christ."

✔ Making My Peace with Mom

The following morning, after getting some sleep, Marie, the kids, and I piled back into the car for the long drive back to Massachusetts for the funeral services. By now, we were all physically and emotionally exhausted.

As I sat at my mother's funeral services, I struggled with so many mixed emotions, including sadness and regret. Sadly, my mother and I never enjoyed the kind of close bond I had with my father.

In looking back, I believe there were several reasons for this. For one thing, Mom had always suffered from depression. This would cause her to retreat from the world and stay isolated in her room. This depressive tendency increased tenfold after my dad's death.

Although my father's death drove my mother deeper into depression than ever, the truth is, she had always been somewhat detached. It was this trait that prevented us from ever forming a close mother-son bond. I know that her serious physical ailments also contributed to her detachment from me.

There was one other deep-seated emotional wound that undoubtedly attributed to my mother's depression. Here's how I found out about it. One day while attending community college and working at St. Luke's Hospital, my mother suddenly appeared in the visitor's lobby of St. Luke's and said she needed to speak with me.

"I need to tell you something," she said. "I was the victim of sexual abuse as a child." Mom had apparently been holding onto that secret forever but was suddenly compelled to talk to me about it. She had withheld this information from my father, undoubtedly out of concern that he might retaliate.

I listened to my mother and comforted her as she cried and shared about the abuse. That same day, Mom would end up sharing this revelation with each of my siblings.

After raising two sons, I now have deeper compassion for my mother. I realize that her physical and emotional ailments proved to be more than she could handle at times. (This burden was certainly more than I knew how to handle as her son). Then there was the grief she carried over losing her husband so young (forty-six), her twenty-eight-year-old son, and her granddaughter who was born with a congenital disease and died at only five years old. (More about that later.)

Mom was a woman of faith; however, her health battles and tragic losses sometimes drove her to thoughts of ending her life. Finally, in death, Mom was at peace and reunited with Dad, Eddie, and other departed loved ones.

✔ Grappling with 9-11

In early 2000, I received a new position within Congressional Affairs, as Liaison to Congress. On September 11th, 2001, I was taking a rare day off to spend quality time with my family. And what a beautiful day it was, with perfect weather.

Marie dropped off the boys and I at a Barnes & Noble bookstore in Fairfax, Virginia and then she headed to the gym for a workout. It was approximately 9:00 a.m. EST when I walked into the bookstore with my boys. I immediately heard an employee say to another from behind the counter. "A plane hit the World Trade Center!"

There was no doubt in my mind that terrorism was behind the attack.

For the moment, I completely ignored what I had heard. I took my boys to the back of the store, grabbed a children's book, and sat on the floor and began reading to them. As I read the words on the pages, my mind raced. I was recalling and mentally reviewing all the dozens of Intelligence Reports (IRs) from the previous months.

I just kept saying to myself, *God, I hope I didn't miss anything or fail to take action!*

Within minutes, I overheard another employee say, "A second plane just hit the World Trade Center!"

My heart sank. I knew that this was no accident. We were now at war. You see, radical Muslim terrorists had issued fatwas (declarations of war) against the U.S years earlier but we ignored them and failed to take the threats seriously.

I knew that our lives were going to change forever once I left our little back corner of the bookstore, our safe haven. So, I stayed and continued reading with the boys until Marie called me, crying.

I took the boys and walked outside to meet Marie. As we drove home, there was the constant sound of sirens, as first responders rushed to various critical infrastructures throughout the Washington D.C. metro area.

Not surprisingly, I was immediately called into work that night. When it was time for me to go to work, a black SUV appeared in my driveway and a fellow agent jumped out. When Marie saw the agent, all geared up in tactical equipment and carrying an automatic weapon, she was frightened.

Both Jacob and Tyler began to ask where I was going and why I was leaving home.

"I love you, Daddy...don't go!" said Jacob. "Bad guys hit the building!"

"I love you, Daddy...don't go!" said Tyler.

Marie and the boys were in tears and worried that something bad could happen to me.

I did my best to reassure them that I would be okay, and promised to be back soon. The truth was, I had no idea how long I would be gone, or when I would be home. The world, and life as we knew it, had been turned upside down.

I kissed them all goodbye, hugged them and told them how much I loved them.

Marie could see the fight in my eyes. "I know you want...need to go," she said. "Just wear your bulletproof vest and be safe."

As I walked outside, another agent handed me an automatic rifle and said, "You may need this."

I looked back toward the house and saw Marie and the boys waving goodbye and blowing kisses.

✔ Understanding Terrorism

When the 9-11 attacks on the World Trade Center occurred, I was horrified and shocked, but I can't say I was surprised. I had seen intelligence in the months prior, and was acutely aware that many within the government had been failing to take the threats seriously for years.

The overall attitude was, "We're America! Acts of international terror only happen in distant, far-off lands like Yemen, Egypt, Israel, Lebanon, and so on. Bad guys wouldn't even dream of harming us!"

This attitude was driven home during the year I had spent in the National Security Division before taking the position in Congressional Affairs. I was chairman of a small terrorism working group across the agency. After the USS Cole attack, I requested a 7:30 a.m. daily intelligence briefing from several personnel.

The general attitude was, "Why have a briefing? We all know they'll never attack us here!"

I was surprised to get push-back over a simple request for a daily briefing—and yet, at the same time, I wasn't surprised. I had seen this laissez-faire attitude spread across most agencies. It is my opinion that this attitude, along with the following factors, converged to create a perfect storm environment for 9-11 to occur:

➤ turf battles between government agencies
➤ lack of intelligence sharing
➤ outdated border computers which track inbound and outbound visitors to the States—computers which were supposed to have been updated years earlier. (Keep in mind that some of the terrorists responsible for 9-11 were here on outdated visas.)

I consider the tragedy of 9-11 to be a total failure by the U.S. government. Prior to 9-11, the United States was completely ignorant of the terror threats, and our overall understanding of Muslims, Arabs and Islam was minimal at best. I do not believe that we have become substantially wiser or more knowledgeable in this regard.

Over the years as an agent, I worked with many Arabs and Muslims in the Gulf States. I found that the majority who practice Islam are good, loving people. They, too, have suffered during this past decade of terror.

Peace-loving Muslims would disavow the statement that the Koran teaches that all the infidels must die. They interpret holy war ("jihad") to mean the internal holy war we all must face as humans—the struggle of good versus evil.

There are, of course, radical Muslims who consider jihad a literal war against non-Muslims, and an imperative to kill. Just as people have done for centuries with the Holy Bible, people interpret the Koran in their own way, and sometimes, sadly, to justify their own means.

Peace-loving Muslims have a moral imperative to report radicalism when and where they encounter it. Radical preaching of the Koran must be reported. And members who hear others speak about Jihad (holy war) in a criminal or terrorist way must report it. Thankfully, through outreach initiatives, the Muslim community has begun to assist law enforcement in its efforts to prevent terror.

When the terrorists recruit and radicalize a new member, they indoctrinate them in several ways, and they keep it up for however long it takes for them to become convinced that the recruit is ready to carry out an attack.

The terrorists have new recruits read the Koran and then interpret it for them in a radical way. They also have recruits watch extremist videos, and often America is demonized in those videos. They brainwash recruits with negative messages like "America is the root of all evil... they're dropping bombs on your family...we need to kill all the infidels...and this is how we do it!"

It is critical to feed your mind good, positive thoughts and surround yourself with good people with good energy. The media has so much influence over the minds of Americans, so be sure the information you're getting from the media is clear, concise and correct. We are all responsible for the information we ingest, just as we are responsible for the food we ingest.

As the saying goes, *As you think, so shall you become.*

✔ Facing Another Family Health Scare

I n the days, weeks and months following 9-11, I and other agents worked around the clock to assist in the investigation and safeguard critical assets from possible sabotage or terrorist acts. And for months afterwards, first responders continued to search the rubble around the World Trade Center and Pentagon, while high-level officials in D.C. and other cities dealt with frightening and deadly Anthrax attacks.

Meanwhile, Marie was about to endure a very personal health shock of her own.

One night, I came home from work and found my wife in bed, sick and in the worst pain I had ever seen her endure. She was feverish, lethargic, disoriented and unable to keep any food down. I checked on her periodically and found that her fever was rising. We couldn't imagine what might be wrong with her.

Marie is a strong Portuguese woman who generally resists going to the doctor or hospital. But after several days had passed without her getting any better, I decided to bring her to the Emergency Room at a local hospital in Fairfax, Virginia. She had the chills and a fever when I brought her in, and she was still in excruciating pain.

After nearly six hours in the E.R. undergoing examination and tests, the attending physician diagnosed Marie with a powerful influenza virus (the flu). After making the diagnosis of a viral infection, the attending physician prescribed Cipro, an antibiotic used to treat severe *bacterial* infections. (Cipro was also the current medicine of choice for those exposed to Anthrax.)

In looking back, I still find this choice of medication baffling. I ask myself, *Why prescribe anti-bacterial medication for a virus?*

The day following the E.R. visit, Marie wasn't showing any improvement so I took her to see her family doctor for another opinion. Unfortunately, her regular doctor was out. So, Marie was examined by an associate who concurred with the E.R. doctor's assessment.

My wife endured two more days and nights of suffering, with her fever spiking to one-hundred-and-four degrees. The skin on her hands began to peel, rashes appeared on her body, and she was disorientated and beginning to panic.

Truth be told, I was beginning to panic as well but I never showed it. I immediately brought her back to her doctor's office.

Thankfully her regular physician was in this time and was able to see her. After a two-minute evaluation, and assessment of her symptoms, he told Marie, "You have toxic shock!" He gave her several shots and sent us back to the E.R. for more intensive treatment.

As I wheeled Marie into the E.R., I saw the same attending physician who had sent her home days earlier. "Hey, Doc! We're back. And guess what? It's not the flu...it's toxic shock. You sent my wife home to die!"

The doctor was in disbelief. So was the E.R. nurse attending to Marie. (This was a different nurse than the one Marie saw on our first visit to the E.R.)

When I explained Marie's health nightmare to the nurse, she looked at me and said, "I've been here for twenty years and I've never seen a toxic shock patient."

"Well, you have now! And the doctor's cavalier attitude nearly cost my wife her life."

Marie was immediately transferred to the I.C.U. Without any family close by to watch the boys, I had to arrange for a sitter. I spent most nights while Marie was in the I.C.U. sleeping in a chair alongside her bed.

It was yet another reminder of how fragile life is, and how everything can change in a New York minute. More importantly, it was a wake-up call and a reminder never to ignore your own instincts and intuition in favor of what a doctor may be saying. A doctor does not live in your skin—only you do. Only *you* truly feel what you are experiencing, health-wise and otherwise. It is important to be switched on and actively involved in your own wellness and medical care.

As Marie spent the entire week in the I.C.U., I spent my days shuttling back and forth between the hospital and home. I brought the boys to see Marie once she was feeling well enough to see them. Even once she was home, it took months for her to fully recover.

In the past, I might have waited to see if Marie's illness cleared up on its own. Eddie's sudden death due to a virus that attacked his heart taught me that it's always better to be safe than sorry. After I lost my twin, I became the kind of person who would seek medical attention right away for myself and my loved ones. I can honestly say that, but not for Eddie's sudden death, Marie very likely may have died at home as well.

✔ Living the Dream at INTERPOL

In January of 2002, I arrived at the pinnacle of my career when I landed a coveted position as a representative at the U.S. National Central Bureau of INTERPOL in Washington, D.C. This was the position dreamed of by most Special Agents.

INTERPOL is the International Criminal Police Organization, and its primary mission is to locate international fugitives and provide intelligence to police organizations throughout the world. INTERPOL is comprised of one-hundred-and-ninety-three member countries and is the second largest international organization after the United Nations. Each country has a central bureau of INTERPOL, and they all report to Headquarters in Lyon, France.

I was based out of D.C. but working with senior agents from across the U.S. Government. Compared to being an agent working the streets, this was a low-stress, life-is-good position. The biggest thing I had to worry about was the paper cuts. I was loving life, working behind a desk, and enjoying coffee and tea breaks twice a day.

Six months into my position, I was asked, along with a few other agents, to go to Headquarters in Lyon to represent the U.S. National Central Bureau of INTERPOL at a terrorist finance conference. The mission of the conference was to identify dirty money from terrorist organizations that raise money for their causes. This was the first INTERPOL conference of this type.

As I was flying over the Atlantic Ocean to the conference, I was listening to Don McLean's song, *Vincent (Starry, Starry Night)* and was deep in reflection.

I felt my father speaking to me internally, saying, *Go home, Eric. Go home…*

Even though my office was in the States, I was assigned to D.C., not to my hometown. I felt like Dad was reminding me of the importance of my family and extended family.

I think Dad was also suggesting I course-correct so I could have a position that was more congruent with my life's purpose—to make this world a little bit better than I found it. I no longer felt I was doing that behind a desk. (It had only taken me six months to tire of my cushy desk job.)

Shortly afterward, I requested a transfer, but it took months to come through. While waiting for my transfer, I continued to be reflective.

One day as I awaited the approval of my transfer, I sat in my office watching the war on terror unfold—footage of the wars in Iraq and Afghanistan. Sitting there, I was thinking about the purpose and meaning of my life.

I asked myself, *Why am I here on this earth? What is my dream, my passion?*

I wanted to be a U.S. Special Agent to make a difference in this world and I wanted to honor my father. I was again reminded that I wasn't accomplishing that by sitting behind a desk. I had become one of those empty suits, sitting in D.C. but not really using the talents God gave me.

I thought to myself, *I am only thirty-eight. I can still contribute. It's time to get off the sidelines and get back into the arena! If that f***ing transfer I requested would just come through!*

In the Spring of 2003, after working at INTERPOL for a little more than a year, I was finally granted my transfer back to the streets—and not just to any office, either. I requested to be transferred to Boston. Home.

Since there were no vacancies at my current level, I voluntarily self-demoted. It was an action most managers frowned upon but, in the end, it was authorized. I was going home after eight years in the New York area and five in Washington, D.C.

In December of 2002, a few days before Christmas, I had Ty on one knee and Jake on the other. They were five and seven. I was having a father-son moment, reminding them of how very blessed we were as a family.

"Remember, boys, we only have one life to live, so we must live it to the fullest!"

Ty, patting me on the shoulder and looking straight into my eyes said, "Yes, Dad, but Jesus had two lives."

I nearly fell to the floor. Even at his young age, my son understood that we will all be born again, like a butterfly, and that we don't have to worry about death. Ty's words reminded me of my father.

✔ Dealing with Another Disappointment

On March 1st, 2003, nine years to the day of Eddie's death, I reported to the Special Agent in Charge, Department of Homeland Security, Immigration & Customs Enforcement, Homeland Security Investigations in Boston. It was a new agency and department stemming from 9-11.

I was assigned to the Strategic Investigations Group, a legacy group within U.S. Customs. This group was investigating individuals and companies attempting to procure WMD materials for countries of concern, or state sponsors of terror.

Within months of arriving, I was transferred into the Legacy INS National Security Group, and once again became a street agent. This transfer wasn't something I was particularly thrilled about and I started questioning whether self-demoting had been the best decision after all my hard work to get to INTERPOL. I had no immigration experience and I preferred the Strategic Investigations Group within Customs because they did the kind of work that interested me—counter-proliferation work.

After an initial few months of feeling uncomfortable in this new role, I began working on a new case. I would spend a couple of years investigating a shipping company that was importing drugs and humans into the United States and allowing wanted felons to flee the U.S. on his vessel. Having latched onto this target, I had a renewed sense of purpose.

Although successful in arresting and deporting an associate of the owner/target who smuggled drugs on the target's container vessel, and himself into the U.S. disguised as a crew member, the U.S. Attorney's Office declined to prosecute, stating that the evidence was insufficient. The owner is still operating today, unfettered, as a shipping company.

I had chased this target for over a year, and the government attorney's failure to prosecute was infuriating and frustrating beyond belief. This case was particularly hard to walk away from but The Serenity Prayer came in handy once again.

✔ The Wicked Good Investigation

On May 12th, 2006, while still working with the Legacy INS National Security Group in Boston, I was asked to review a tip that was called into our tip line by an anonymous caller. The tip was related to a business in New Bedford, Massachusetts identified as Michael Bianco Inc. (MBI).

The caller alleged that the owner of MBI, Francesco Insolia, an Italian immigrant, was knowingly hiring hundreds of illegal aliens and assisting many with obtaining fake or fraudulent identification documents.

The tipster described deplorable working conditions at MBI. These included: providing only one roll of toilet paper per stall per day; docking an employee's pay by fifteen minutes for every minute they were late; fining employees twenty dollars for spending more than two minutes in a restroom stall; and terminating them for a subsequent offense; fining employees twenty dollars for leaving their work area before the sounding of the bell signaling the break; fining employees twenty dollars for talking while working; and terminating them for additional violations.

What stood out was the fact that the company was a Department of Defense (DOD) contractor that manufactured tactical military vests.

It was later discovered that Insolia's wife was the president of a company called Front Line Defense (FLD) which operated out of the same facility. The way MBI did business was to have workers clock in and out on MBI timecards for all hours between 8:00 a.m. and 5:00 p.m. and then clock back in on FLD timecards, to avoid overtime compensation.

Based on my training and experience, several red flags were raised immediately. I harked back to the ESC case, where we had a defense contractor physically offshoring production of goods and services to Russia. In this case, Insolia simply brought the foreign workers to the U.S. to make the goods.

This had broad national security implications. I knew that if terrorists had found their way into the defense contractor's facility, we might be dealing with serious injuries and/or death. I also knew that terrorists could infiltrate and sabotage these goods by, let's say, rubbing a WMD agent like ricin on the vests, potentially resulting in the deaths of our military service members.

Some people would say, "No way...that could never happen!" It most certainly could, as terrorists are limited only by their imaginations.

Utilizing law enforcement technology, I was able to track down the anonymous caller and cultivate her into assisting in the investigation as a Confidential Informant (CI). CIs are the lifeline of any street agent. They are in a position to provide the who, what, when, where and how of a criminal organization. They can be pivotal in ensuring that we can successfully investigate and prosecute. Confidential Informants could be anyone from ex-spouses of criminals, to competitors who see unfair practices, to concerned citizens.

This particular CI was a female and a mother and the perfect example of a concerned citizen type of CI. She was motivated by the desire to do the right thing—but she also had skin in the game because MBI employed her as a stitcher. She was shocked that the owner had so many illegal workers employed, and furious that these positions weren't available to the residents of New Bedford.

This was a sad state of affairs for New Bedford, which had the highest unemployment rate in the state. MBI had received approximately fifty-seven-thousand dollars in tax incentives to hire legal citizens. Hundreds and hundreds of legal U.S. citizens could have and should have been employed by MBI with that money. They could have attracted workers not only from Massachusetts but from the neighboring states of New Hampshire, Rhode Island and New York—people who were willing to relocate to work for a good defense contractor.

MBI could have offered legal U.S. citizens the kind of employment opportunities that would have enabled them to buy groceries, put their kids through school and buy a home. There is a residual benefit to the economy when you have a corporation hiring legal citizens.

I asked myself, *How could this be happening, with this many alleged illegal aliens in one business? Surely, during DOD visits, they witnessed the deplorable conditions and spoke to workers. So, where was the DOD oversight of this business? Didn't anybody ask the right questions? Didn't anybody from local, state or federal government care?*

As the investigation continued, it would become clear that an attitude of willful blindness hovered over the entire city.

The fact that all this was happening in my hometown of New Bedford was hard to swallow. New Bedford had been considered one of the wealthiest cities in America during the whaling days (as depicted in Moby Dick). Now it was one of the worst cities in America.

Over the past several decades, the elected officials of my hometown had failed this once beautiful city. They had poured billions of dollars into the town with little to show for it. They allowed poverty and crime to continue unabated to the point that New Bedford had been for many years one of the worst cities in the state as far as crime was concerned. The schools had been labeled as underperforming by the state, factories once bustling had closed, and street crime and opium drug use was the highest in the state.

Even the air quality had suffered—as it still does today. (Findings from a May, 2017 study done by the University of Iowa and Boston University of Public Health showed that airborne PCB emissions from the New Bedford Harbor constitute the single largest continuous source of airborne PCB ever measured from natural waters in the U.S. and Canada. That is a very disturbing statistic.)

Once a city or corporation gets a reputation for being welcoming of illegal aliens, word quickly gets out that, "As long as you make it to New Bedford, Massachusetts, you'll have a job. No one there really cares about your immigration status." Illegal aliens then start coming in great numbers, via whatever means of transport is available—planes, trains, automobiles, etc.

That was exactly what happened with MBI. Word got out that they were a safe haven corporation and illegal alien workers started showing up on their doorstep. And then, thanks to local, state and federal government officials turning a blind eye, MBI was able to continue to operate.

This is globalization totally run amok! I thought.

Globalization is supposed to be such a positive thing for America— but it is like catnip to transnational criminal groups, enabling them to exploit trade, travel and telecommunication. Sadly, governments, including the U.S., haven't put sufficient measures in place that would stop transnational criminals from using globalization to their advantage and our detriment.

This case was right up my alley and I grabbed onto it like a wild dog with a bone. The case I had been waiting for, in my very own hometown.

✔ Uncovering the Political Motivations

With the awarding of DOD contracts worth hundreds of millions of dollars to one of this depressed city's largest employers, one would have expected the Mayor to make a public announcement promoting his city and congratulating MBI.

So, I asked myself, *Why wouldn't the Mayor want to show its citizens, its politicians, and others in the state that New Bedford was getting millions in government contracts and putting people to work?*

Yet, there was no such announcement and no press release. Something didn't add up.

The only reason I could come up with for the Mayor's silence was politics. From my perspective, the Mayor had to have known that MBI was involved in illegal operations. But no democratic mayor would want to upset the Democratic Party and put themselves in a position where they were denied funding come reelection time.

After all, Massachusetts was a democratic state and New Bedford was now an unofficial sanctuary city. (The Democratic Party was in support of both illegal aliens and sanctuary cities.) Anything that went against that value system would have upset the Democratic Party. The world of politics can feel like the Mafia in the sense that either you're in or you're out. There's no gray area.

Even the Catholic Church in New Bedford accepted the influx of illegal aliens. In 2004 with its membership dwindling, my family's home parish, St. James Church, renamed itself Our Lady of Guadalupe Parish at St. James to appeal to a new Hispanic group of members.

Ironically on May 15th, within days of the anonymous tip coming in concerning MBI, President George W. Bush addressed the nation to discuss "a matter of national importance"—the reform of America's immigration system.

I immediately thought of the anonymous tip and the New Bedford defense contractor allegedly hiring hundreds of illegal aliens to manufacture defense goods for the U.S. military.

As President Bush outlined his five goals, he mentioned his support for the temporary work program where foreign workers would be matched with willing American employers for "jobs Americans are not doing."

The implication of his statement was clear, and there were subsequent statements that were even clearer.

I was shocked. I asked myself, *Did the president just say what I think I heard him say—that Americans are turning down job opportunities because they're lazy?*

I wanted to shout at the T.V., "Americans would surely do those jobs Mr. President! And you need to fire the advisor who managed to get that line into your speech!"

Again, I wondered, *What has happened to my country, my city?*

✔ Becoming Manager of the Wicked Good Case

A couple of months into the development of the MBI case, which I had initiated, I was promoted upstairs to oversee the entire case in a managerial and supervisory capacity. Meanwhile, a senior agent with years of experience and expertise was appointed as case agent, with me as his boss. After self-demoting to return to the streets, I was now given my grade back.

When I was a street agent, I was responsible for my individual cases. As a manager, I was responsible for the entire squad. Now, I had influence over the squad in terms of the direction it was heading, the type of cases we would take on, and who to arrest and prosecute, or not. I was in my element and I found it very fulfilling.

I was now the supervisor of all the National Security Division cases at the time, but MBI was my baby. I lived with it on a daily basis.

The newly assigned case agent continued to identify all the illegal aliens while other agents were planning and arranging the introduction into MBI of a UCA posing as an illegal alien. A recording of a bad guy admitting to his crime would prove to be powerful evidence for a jury.

The CI was able to provide us not only the who, what and where but she took it to the next level. She went into the office manager's office and said, "Hey, I have a friend who needs a job," thereby setting the stage for our undercover operation.

The undercover office division maintained dossiers on all our certified Undercover Special Agents. These dossiers were kept top secret, of course, to protect the UCAs. After all, a UCA is getting a whole new identity, from passport to driver's license. (Being a UCA sounds very exciting and glamorous until you take into account the extreme risks they have to take.)

I was sent dossiers of several UCAs, and I spent some time reviewing them and interviewing several candidates. Ultimately, I selected a female Spanish-speaking UCA from Texas.

(As I mentioned earlier, I never became certified as an Undercover Special Agent because I knew I was a terrible liar and not cut out for the work. I occasionally did very limited undercover operations but with anything more involved, we brought in an experienced and certified UCA.)

The case agent and I spent hours briefing the UCA on the entire case, and we provided dossiers on the targets. In addition, the UCA spent time getting to know the CI who dropped the dime on the bad guys.

On September 7th, 2006, nearly a dozen agents and the UCA met in a hotel room in an adjacent city. The tech agent provided a phone which would be recording and transmitting the conversations to listening agents, who would also be recording. Before show time, another agent would doublecheck to make sure the UCA wasn't in possession of her credentials, badge or weapon.

The cover team was in position and the green light was given to the UCA to proceed into MBI. Protecting the UCA was paramount. So, the cover team monitored her every move and listened to the transmission for any word of trouble—the sign that they needed to immediately move in to extract her. With over five hundred people in this building, the majority of whom were illegal and some of whom were criminals, the team had to be on their toes and ready to move.

Posing as an illegal alien, the UCA entered MBI and had direct recorded conversations with Insolia, his managers and coworkers. The UCA provided them with a Mexican I.D. and verbally confirmed that she was a Mexican national, not a U.S. resident or citizen, and in fact illegally present in the U.S. (a necessary element of the violations).

MBI accepted the UCA as an employee, knowing that she was an illegal alien. Then they instructed her to obtain fraudulent documents at a business across the street from MBI. An employee of this business was previously arrested and, on July 26th, 2004 in New York City, convicted of possession of forged documents.

Yet, this same employee was now back at work a year later. He charged the UCA one-hundred-and-twenty dollars for a counterfeit Social Security card and counterfeit Alien Registration card in a fake name. These IDs would be presented and accepted as authentic, even though MBI management not only knew these documents were fake, but were the ones who instructed the UCA to obtain them.

We learned a shocking fact: since 2002, the Social Security Administration (SSA) had been sending correspondence to MBI, informing the company that many of the Social Security numbers that MBI provided to SSA pursuant to annual reporting requirements appeared to be fraudulent or invalid.

In February of 2007, MBI submitted six-hundred-and-forty-six W-2 payroll records for the tax year 2006. Of those, the SSA determined that four-hundred-and-twenty-eight—more than 66% of the records submitted!—were deficient in some manner. This was a staggering number.

Days later after passing the sewing test, the UCA was officially hired at MBI. Prior to starting work one particular day, she spoke to two males who said they were in the United States without papers and had no form of identification. The UCA subsequently learned that an office manager hired both men.

Demonstrating knowledge of the illegal aliens working at the company, an MBI manager shared with the UCA the fact that many workers from Honduras and Guatemala had paid five-to-six-thousand dollars to smugglers to get them to MBI.

At the same time, other agents were systematically planning the overall execution of the arrests and search warrants, and setting up the immigration processing center we would use to process the illegal aliens after arresting them.

✔ Diverting My Attention to Religious Worker Fraud

As the MBI investigation was proceeding nicely, I needed to divert my attention to another case. (I, and most other managers, had to multitask.) One of the agents in the group I managed was detailed to the FBI's Joint Terrorism Task Force (JTTF), and was spearheading an investigation into a nationwide "religious worker visa" scheme with ties to the terrorist group LeT (Lashkar-e-Taiba), operating out of Pakistan.

(In Urdu, Lashkar-e-Taiba literally means "Army of the good" and is often translated to mean "Army of the righteous" or "Army of the pure.") LeT was the group responsible for the Mumbai hotel attacks which began on November 26th of 2008, lasted about a week, and killed one-hundred-and-sixty-four people.

So, there I was, deep into the MBI case, as one of the biggest national security raids in U.S. history was about to take place. At the same time, I was working this other national security case involving members of LeT. Needless to say, trying to practice SEE and get a decent night of sleep was not easy.

This operation targeted illegal aliens trying to fraudulently enter the U.S. on religious-worker visas. Here's how their scheme worked:

Let's say a foreign-born individual living in Pakistan wanted to come to the U.S. They would go to the American Embassy and say, in essence, "I am an imam* and here is my document proving it…" (*A Muslim priest.)

Then that individual would show documents proving that they had gone to a certain university. They would also submit letters of recommendation from Pakistan as well as letters of invitation from the U.S. stating that they had been asked to come serve as the imam at a certain mosque. All the documents and letters were forged.

In this case, the so-called religious workers were actually fraudsters posing as imams. In at least one of these cases, the fraudulent imam was connected to LeT.

Whether or not the mosques which had supposedly invited these fraudsters to come serve as imams was also in question. In some instances, the mosques were colluding with the fraudsters and in other instances, the mosques didn't realize that the supposed imams were not legitimate, and got duped as well.

On November 15th, 2006, after months of preparation and coordination with agents from around the nation, Homeland Security and FBI Agents arrested thirty-three Pakistanis who received religious-worker visas to enter the United States but were in fact fraudsters.

Several imams in the Boston area were arrested. One subject arrested was Muhammed Hafiz Masood whose brother is the leader of LeT. Interestingly, only weeks earlier, I had sat in a mosque with Muhammed Hafiz Masood and shared a meal as part of a U.S. Government outreach program to the Muslim community called Bridges.

There were many Muslim people in the room and as we sat, other agents and I made eye contact with Mr. Masood. We were sitting at this table, scanning the room, and we recognized Masood as someone we had been investigating for about a year.

Media reports state that Masood is living in Pakistan today after pleading guilty in Boston Federal Court to immigration fraud. That's right—the U.S. Government decided to merely deport Masood rather than criminally prosecute him in Federal Court.

For the life of me, I couldn't understand why the government attorneys wouldn't have prosecuted him. I could only imagine that it once again came down to political considerations combined with prosecutorial timidity.

The ongoing situation at Guantanamo Bay teaches us about complexity in this regard. Many people from America, and the Middle Eastern countries whose citizens we are detaining, have been asking for years why nothing has been done, and why we have been holding these detainees in limbo for so long.

Let's take a look at the options.

The U.S. could try these enemy combatants in Federal Court—but would we have the necessary evidence to prove guilt beyond a reasonable doubt, and convict?

And if the trial did take place in Federal Court, the attorneys would be required to abide by Federal Regulations and Rules of Evidence, including the requirement that the defendants be tried by a jury or their peers. Where would we find a jury of their peers?

Then there is the option to deport the detainees instead. But, what if we sent them back to their countries of origins, or a neighboring country, and they got right back into the fight and resumed terrorist activities?

We must also consider the politics of the situation. The U.S. is always measured in any proposed course of action against the Gulf States. While it might be a stretch to consider some Gulf States outright allies, we tend to have a cordial if tenuous relationship with them that we might not want to jeopardize. The United Arab Emirates (UAE), for example, allows us to house and base some of our vessels there, and Saudi Arabia and Qatar offer similar military support by allowing us to house military equipment and personnel in the region unimpeded.

In some cases, we are upsetting the Gulf State governments anyway. Their feeling is that we should either charge the Guantanamo detainees with a crime or let them go. (I wholeheartedly agree.) The United States would be saying the same thing if the roles were reversed.

The reality is that from the U.S. Government's perspective, there are no good options. So, we have elected to classify these detainees as enemy combatants, giving us the authority to hold then indefinitely in military limbo at Guantanamo Bay.

✔ Gearing Up for the Wicked Good Raid

The time had come at last for our raid on MBI.

By this time, we had briefed the Secretary of Public Safety (the Governor's righthand man), the Mayor, the Massachusetts State Police, and all other government entities that might have been impacted by the raid.

With so many illegal aliens in one building, the element of surprise was key to safely and successfully executing this operation. All out-of-state agents were sequestered about sixty miles away in the metro Boston area, cautioned about limiting communications, and reminded to make sure operational security measures were strictly enforced.

There were many agents in on the operation, and we could not afford one slip-up. We didn't want an agent inadvertently leaving the operational plan they were reviewing laying around in their hotel room where prying eyes could see it...or leaving it in a restaurant...or a restroom. And the last thing we needed was for an agent to have one too many at the hotel bar one night and start blabbing to a beautiful stranger, "Hey, I'm a Federal Agent and we're about to execute a big raid!"

Just one agent who was switched off instead of on could have torpedoed our operation before it ever got off the ground. So, we reminded everyone of the old adage, "Loose lips sink ships!"

Before dawn on March 6th, 2007, the morning of the operation, I visited the gravesites of my parents and Eddie, who are buried together.

It was a windy, bone chilling day, with seven-degree temperatures and wind gusts lowering the temperature even more.

As I said a prayer and mentioned the impending raid, I envisioned Eddie smiling and asking "Can I come...please?" I envisioned my father telling me how proud he was of my service to our country. And I could almost hear my mom saying, "Be safe!"

I thanked them for inspiring me, lifting me up when I was down and helping me carry the burden of life on the hard days.

Then I left and went directly to the NBPD to brief officers who would be assisting in the raid. It was another pinch-yourself moment. This was the same Police Department where my dad worked for nearly eighteen years before his sudden death.

As I stood before them, I encouraged safety and professionalism and mentioned that this raid would be closely monitored by the Department of Homeland Security and would probably get news coverage. Little did I know that this case would be on the front page of most papers in the U.S., including The Washington Post and The New York Times, and get the attention of the White House and specifically the president.

I left the Police Department and rendezvoused with the seventy-five-car motorcade to initiate and coordinate the multi-site search and arrest operation. As we were getting ready to roll, I needed to make sure all agents were set.

The motorcade was ready and every agent knew their assignment. The surveillance team at MBI was in place and reporting that the target location was clear and ready for us. The arrest team at the owner's home was in place and ready to take him down. And agents at the document vendor's place of business were ready.

Meanwhile, a Coast Guard helicopter would be our eyes in the sky, an NBPD tactical team was standing by, and a NBPD water vessel would be in the water, ready to rescue any illegal aliens who tried to flee over the hurricane barriers protecting the city against flooding.

✔ Trusting in God—and Our Preparations

W e were ready to execute. It was just after 8:00 a.m.

I was in the lead vehicle in the front right seat, coordinating with our command post as we made the thirty-minute ride. As we travelled, I received communication that the owner was arrested without incident as he left his home. So far, so good.

We were traveling about a twenty-five-mile route from the rendezvous location to the target location. With that many cars, we needed an escort to make sure our motorcade was tight and would arrive intact and safely.

Massachusetts State Police and NBPD officers escorted us and did an excellent job of blocking onramps and offramps as we proceeded down to the target location. We had uniformed police with us in the motorcade and a command center bus, as well—mostly undercover covert vehicles. Of course, the police escort was a dead giveaway. We also had our blue lights ("wig-wags") flashing on our grills.

The newspaper later quoted people watching us roll by, as saying, "I wondered what the hell was going on. And I asked myself, 'Are they looking for Osama bin Laden? Are we at war? Or what in the world is happening to have this many police vehicles rolling by at once?'"

Quite frankly, our show of force was not overkill, considering that MBI employed about five hundred illegal aliens, some of whom were convicted criminals. We couldn't predict what might happen once we got inside the facility, or what the reaction to our presence might be.

Desperate people do desperate things. Traditionally and historically speaking, illegal aliens tend to be runners who do not obey Law Enforcement Officers, and are prepared to fight if necessary. They tend to be people who are desperate to stay in America and are willing to do, and risk, whatever it takes to escape capture. In the process, they put at risk the lives of Law Enforcement Officers who are simply working to enforce laws enacted by our politicians.

I decided to put the car radio on for just a moment during a lull in the action, and as I did, Earth Wind & Fire's *Boogie Wonderland* came on. Earth, Wind & Fire was Eddie's favorite band and hearing them, I felt like my brother and father were watching over me. It gave me inspiration and comfort and brought back great memories from Emery Street, only blocks from the target.

When we were five minutes out from MBI, the chatter over the radio came to a halt. There was a solemnity in the air and it was palpable.

Everyone knew that with this many illegal aliens at the target location, something was bound to happen. We all knew we were risking our lives to execute this operation and we didn't know what the outcome was going to be, or how many of us would still be standing afterwards. We were Law Enforcement Officers, but in that moment, we may as well have been firemen about to enter a burning building.

I was also aware from my experience in Washington, D.C. and my time in Congressional Affairs that this raid had political legs and would resonate, one way or another, with the media. Immigration was such a hot-topic issue. I couldn't possibly have known just how big a media explosion this raid was going to cause.

All I could do was say a prayer, have faith in myself and my fellow agents, and believe that everyone was well prepared and practiced in carrying out this type of operation. We had spent months in planning and preparations. We always trained and prepared extensively because we knew better than to try to make sound decisions with adrenaline coursing through our blood.

In times of crisis and chaos, both the body and mind shut down due to the adrenaline surge that comes from being in fight-or-flight mode. The mind goes blank—unless it has previously been trained to react. Once you find yourself in a crisis event, it is too late to think of a plan of action. Your only hope is your memory bank.

In the heat of battle, the training kicks in at the very moment your conscious mind fails you due to adrenaline rushes and fear. Your mind will automatically retrieve the plan you've rehearsed, assuming that there is a plan in place to retrieve. If you're well trained, then the body will potentially follow—and both mind and body will be safe.

Train enough and then, when the shit hits the fan, you're ready to rock and roll. So, we conducted quarterly drills, varying the conditions. Sometimes we would do drills in daylight and sometimes in the dark. Sometimes we would train inside and sometimes outside. We simulated active shooting situations with paintball guns. If we were doing an indoor drill, we would go into a house and go through the motions of executing warrants and arrests, and shoot each other with paintballs.

We would simulate take-cover and concealment techniques. We were trained to instantaneously spot and recognize the kind of objects indoors and out that provide the best cover. Indoors, walls and partitions are best—or any barrier made of brick or metal. (Wood and fabric—couches and cushions—are not your friends in a gunfire situation.) Outdoors, there are many more options than indoors including telephone posts, metal garbage dumpsters and vehicle engine blocks, to name a few.

There is a saying among Law Enforcement Officers: If you fail to prepare, prepare to fail. So, as agents, we were constantly training our minds and bodies for these types of events. We could not afford to freeze and find ourselves unable to function. We had to be fully switched on.

✔ Executing the Wicked Good Raid

W e were now sixty seconds from showtime, or "Alpha Out" as it was known by us agents. One minute later, we were given the go signal from the surveillance vehicle at MBI. The Chief of NBPD had a medical vehicle standing by for us, just in case.

My driver was a Captain for the Massachusetts State Police. As we approached, he looked at me, shook my hand, and said, "Good luck. Sorry we can't go in with you."

"Wait…what?" I couldn't believe my ears. I was stunned.

It turned out that a week before the raid, word came down that Massachusetts State Police had been told by the Governor, "Listen, guys…I know you've been helping on the investigation and planning and everything. And you can escort the agents to the location…but don't you dare go into the building and search the premises or arrest any illegal aliens!"

The Governor didn't want any of his guys to be seen entering the facility or escorting illegal aliens. It was entirely a political decision made by a democratic, pro-illegal alien Governor. It would have looked bad for him to be involved in a roundup of illegal aliens.

The five hundred souls in the building were comprised of approximately half men and half women, including some eighty illegal aliens with previous deportation orders and several with criminal records. These were people who had already gone through the system and been told to leave but didn't. We weren't going after priests and nuns here.

As I entered MBI, I saw the eyes of hundreds and hundreds of third-world-nation people, all slaving away. They were gaunt and looked sickly. It didn't look like they had been eating regularly or well. They looked worn down from constantly sitting at tables, slaving away, making U.S. military goods.

It was like a scene right out of *The Jungle*, a 1906 novel that portrayed the harsh working conditions and exploited lives of immigrants in the United States. In the movie, these elements were contrasted with the deeply-rooted corruption of people of power. Little did I know in that moment just how much of a correlation there was between the situation at hand and *The Jungle*. The similarities would prove staggering.

It was a holy shit moment.

I thought, *What the hell is going on here? These poor bastards are being abused! We have a sweat-shop environment right here on American soil and the U.S. Government is doing contracts with them! How in the world does this happen in the building of a U.S. defense contractor?*

My immediate reaction when I saw the working conditions was, *This can't be real! Not in my country, my state, my city!*

But it was real, and I was about to stop it.

At my direction, a Spanish-speaking agent announced over the intercom to shut all machines off and not to run. But, of course, within seconds of the announcement, workers began to run.

I quickly ordered the rest of my team inside.

One pregnant worker collapsed and one agent fell up the stone stairs, cracking his head open.

Then I heard someone announce over the radio, "We have a barricade situation in the bathroom!"

In preparation for this day, we had the SWAT team standing by, a half mile away in a covert location, ready to deploy if we needed them. We hadn't wanted to inflame things further by entering with them.

I told my NBPD liaison to have the SWAT team get ready to deploy. Within minutes, the situation was brought under control and the SWAT team was told to stand down.

Each detainee was taken to the immigration processing center we had set up, and extensively interviewed. For humanitarian reasons, thirty-five illegal aliens were released from MBI with an immigration order. Dozens more would follow in the days following the operation.

Within the hour, the situation was well under control and all agents were busy carrying out their assigned duties. Then I received word that the local radio station was reporting that some workers had possibly run up and over the hurricane barriers into the frigid water.

I thought, *God, no!*

The report back from the police vessel in the water was, "No bodies in the water."

All I could do was thank the NBPD Chief for offering the police vessel.

Under my supervision, the National Security Squad, with support from nearly three hundred DHS personnel and over a hundred state and local officers, had pulled off one of the largest mass arrests in U.S. history at a single location—a U.S. defense contractor. Another several hundred more agents and staff were busy processing the illegal aliens at the established immigration processing center.

I thought it was a "wicked good" operation, as we say in Boston.

What else could I have thought? After all, we had successfully arrested three-hundred-and-sixty-one illegal aliens out of five hundred employees, criminally arrested the owner and two of his managers, executed a search warrant at this business, and arrested an individual producing counterfeit identifications—an individual who happened to be illegally present in the United States himself.

Throughout the day, agents discovered illegal aliens hiding in boxes in the four-story brick factory where MBI was housed. The place was approximately 161,709 square feet and sat on over four acres of land, so there was no shortage of places to hide.

✔ Feeling Betrayed in the Wicked Aftermath

On March 7th, 2007, at 6:00 a.m., the morning after the Wicked Good Raid, I heard my cell phone ringing. I had only had a few hours of sleep.

It was the Special Agent in Charge (SAC), Bruce Foucart, another guy from New Bedford. Ironically, we grew up just a few streets away from each other and close to the target business.

I knew that the SAC wasn't calling to congratulate me. Before heading to bed the night before, I had witnessed the beginnings of the intense media backlash. The media was claiming that MBI was a handbag plant full of women, which was patently false.

While watching *The O'Reilly Factor* (Bill O'Reilly's show on Fox News), I saw the narrative quickly turn. The raid was first described as a DOJ defense contractor/critical infrastructure/national security operation but now it was a "humanitarian crisis," as described by the governor.

I told Marie, "The case is about to go south!" And I was right.

Now, the Massachusetts Congressional Delegation was calling for a DHS Office of Inspector General investigation on how and why the case was executed. And the SAC was calling to talk to me about the raid and the blowback.

During the call, the SAC said that the Department of Homeland Security was getting barraged with questions from the White House. He needed stats from me: how many males/females had been arrested; how many had been released from MBI for humanitarian reasons the day of the raid; how many were released from the immigration processing center.

After spending five years working in D.C., I knew how things worked. The White House calls DHS, which then calls Immigrations & Customs Enforcement. Politics and the media were now driving the case.

We had conducted our operation with oversight from the DHS, and after nearly a year of detailed planning, we had done exactly what we said we were going to do.

The DHS *knew perfectly well* what we were setting out to do and were in fact in charge of it. But, because they now had to defend themselves, they went into micromanagement mode. They were picking apart our entire operation and questioning every move we had made. It was clear that their loyalties had shifted.

The SAC explained that the very same administration that was pushing for tougher immigration policies was also embarrassed that we had hit a U.S. Department of Defense contractor. The operation didn't fit the narrative of the President, and most democratic politicians, that, "Illegal aliens are simply doing jobs Americans won't do."

In truth, The New Bedford Standard Times ran an article weeks later showing hundreds of New Bedford citizens waiting for job interviews at MBI. A prospective worker was quoted as saying that "I would love to have a job with the DOD supporting our military in Iraq and Afghanistan."

On the one hand, the article was coming out against our operation. On the other hand, the article supported our operation by showing New Bedford residents standing in line waiting for a job.

Why was my department being pounded by the wicked aftermath?

The illegal aliens employed by MBI came to America and entered unlawfully. They did not follow the rules required of people around the world if they want to live and work in America. We are a nation of laws and unless we want to become a third-world country, we need to enforce our laws.

I understood how the desperation of the illegal aliens working at MBI drove them to break the law in hopes of living better lives. In so doing, they put themselves in position to be exploited.

Many people said, "Well, the conditions in their homeland are worse, so this is the lesser of two evils!"

I said that our immigration laws state that illegal aliens have to go back to where they came from and apply for legal entry, amnesty or a work visa. And, I would add that our laws state that illegal aliens have to wait their turn, like all lawful people from around the world do, often waiting five or ten years to get to America legally.

The branch of government that employed me was in charge of enforcing our immigration laws. The system is not perfect but we have procedures in place that have been in place for many years—and these procedures are there for valid reasons, including our safety.

If our elected officials don't like these procedures, they need to change them. It is unfair to hire Law Enforcement Officers to enforce laws and procedures—and then turn on us when we do what we were hired to do.

We were hired to do a job and we did it—with *the blessing* of the Department of Homeland Security!

✔ Getting Pounded by the Wicked Aftermath

MBI had been awarded two-hundred-and-thirty-million dollars' worth of government contracts since 2004, and the majority of its workforce were illegal foreign workers. The Defense Logistics Agency noted that MBI was one of the top defense contractors in the U.S.— number eighty-two out of one hundred, to be exact.

DOD inspectors visited MBI, and in fact had an office onsite!

Insolia was quoted as saying, "Inspectors interacted with our workers without incident or complaint."

The inspector didn't report any labor problems because he didn't know they existed. He was told by management that the Hispanics he saw on the factory floor were hired by an employment agency.

The illegal aliens were being portrayed as victims, and they were. They had been exploited by MBI, and treated like slave labor rather than human beings. Insolia was responsible for that but the U.S. Government turned a blind eye to it.

But what about the citizens of New Bedford who didn't have an opportunity for good DOD jobs? They were victims too—the forgotten victims in the wicked aftermath.

The media, along with the local, state and federal democratic elected officials were all determined to set a different narrative and demonize the men and woman of Homeland Security. In their eyes, this was a "wicked bad" operation, not a wicked good operation, as I believed it to be.

There was even a "How dare you!" outcry from the Catholic Church. During the homilies at the masses following the Wicked Good Raid, I would hear priests pray for the undocumented workers affected by what they essentially called "the massive Nazi government raids."

Yet, I never heard one priest pray for the men and women of law enforcement. No priests prayed for me and my family or mentioned how we had sacrificed for years to keep America safe. It was fine for priests to pray for the illegal aliens, but there was no love shown for us Law Enforcement Officers who were simply trying to enforce the laws we had sworn to enforce.

The disinformation campaign was in full swing. Meanwhile, the government held half as many press conferences as the media, and did a poor job of getting out in front of the story concerning the national security implications of MBI.

It was disheartening and demoralizing to know that my own government and agency was failing to stand up for us and aggressively tell the story of what had actually occurred. They didn't come out in the media and state unequivocally that this was about national security.

That was the bottom line and that was the drum we should have been hitting from day one. Instead, we got all twisted up in the wicked aftermath. We were so busy answering the mail from the White House, the media, and the Catholic Church, so to speak, that we took our eye off the ball.

Headquarters was controlling the SAC's interaction with the media, and was operating under the naïve assumption that the media frenzy would blow over.

In preparation for a pending press conference days before the operation, I had suggested to the U.S. Attorney's office that we utilize MBI Grand Jury exhibits which included photos of the tactical flight vests manufactured by MBI and worn by U.S. fighter pilots and other servicemen in Iraq and Afghanistan. I had felt that it was important that the media and public understand that national security was at the very heart of this case. Unfortunately, my advice fell on deaf ears.

I would simply ask the citizens of New Bedford this question: "Has turning a blind eye to illegal aliens, with all the residual crime and costs that flows from that, helped your city prosper over the decade? Who has it empowered, other than politicians and nongovernmental organizations?"

Anyone can stand up and make great speeches, saying, "We should all be inclusive!"

✔ Reconciling the Wicked Aftermath

Immigration advocacy groups and politicians were fabricating stories and telling half truths about the operation. The media, an independent vital feature of any liberal democracy, must act as an effective check on government power and provide people with accurate and impartial information so they can act accordingly.

In this case, they failed miserably to uphold this tradition.

The South Coast Today newspaper (the former New Bedford Standard Times) ran front-page stories on the case for years, coming out as critical of DHS efforts. In so doing, they were unknowingly attacking the same agent they had glorified in 1998 as a "son of New Bedford who would make the forefathers of our country proud."

Given that the similarities between the ESC case and the MBI case were so obvious, it was hard to believe I had been painted with such vastly different brushes by the media on these two cases. The only real difference in the cases was that in the ESC case, the defense contractor was offshoring the production of military equipment to foreign countries, and in the MBI case, illegal foreign workers were brought to the U.S. to manufacture the goods.

Then there was The Washington Post article that ran on Sunday, March 18th, 2007, entitled "Immigration Raid Rips Families."

The article stated that a Maria Escoto from Honduras, who paid a "coyote" to make the fifteen-day journey to New Bedford, wasn't allowed to make a phone call for three days after her arrest, leaving her young children unaware of her whereabouts.

The story went on to say that, supposedly, other children were suffering without their arrested parents, as well. These included a seven-year-old who called a DHS hotline, looking for her mother, and a breastfeeding baby who refused a bottle and was hospitalized for dehydration. The article continued by stating that the Governor categorized the raid as a humanitarian crisis.

Interestingly, Ms. Escoto was quoted as saying that she was aware of similar raids but assumed that since MBI was working on government contracts, she would be "safe from a raid."

The article ended with Ms. Escoto being released with an ankle bracelet and being issued an immigration court date. The reporter failed to corroborate or contact DHS officials for comments.

I always understood that the basic rule of journalism was to talk to all sides. Or, at least that's what was preached in my journalism course at Northeastern. Evidently, this was not followed at the premier Washington Post. The Deputy National Editor, Steve Holmes later admitted that failing to call officials was, "a bad error on all our parts."

In fact, Ms. Escoto *did* make a phone call the evening of her arrest and was released. We were never able to confirm that a seven-year-old called the established hotline, or that a dehydrated baby was hospitalized.

The wicked aftermath in the MBI case brought to mind this Winston Churchill quote: "A lie gets halfway around the world before the truth has a chance to get its pants on."

All these years later I still find it astonishing that not a single news outlet asked about or investigated the national security question. And yet, at the very heart of the MBI case was our national security.

If we haven't learned the most basic lesson from 9-11—the fact that terrorists are limited only by their imagination—then we as a nation are doomed for another attack like 9-11. Only, next time it will be much, much worse.

Let us not forget the victims of 9-11 and all those souls who have been slaughtered by terrorist groups.

Let us not forget the Fall of 2001 when five people died and seventeen were sickened by anthrax.

History proves that germ warfare has been used for thousands of years. The British gave American Indians blankets and handkerchiefs infected with smallpox. The Russians, U.S., British and Germans all have some type of germ warfare programs.

If a terrorist could find his or her way into a U.S. defense contractor's facility to commit acts of sabotage, like placing a chemical nerve agent like ricin, capable of killing all whose skin it touched, why wouldn't they? Or, if terrorists were able to place tracking devices on these MBI vests so adversaries could monitor our soldiers' location and then kill them, why wouldn't they?

Who ever imagined that nineteen foreign "students" and visitors would hijack U.S. planes, kill the pilots and fly them into our national symbols? Until it actually happened, this idea seemed foolish and crazy and sounded like the imaginings of a fiction writer like Tom Clancy.

✔ Handling the Wicked Political Machinery

I could understand the death threats I got from the MS-13 gang, the protest marches, and the rallies held, ironically, at my high school and at my family parish, St. James Church. What I found most disheartening was how the politicians—the Mayor, the Governor, and Senators Kennedy and Kerry—all flocked to New Bedford like ambulance-chasing lawyers, salivating over the opportunity to pose for photos with a crying baby or the child of one of the illegal aliens taken into custody.

Kennedy said, "The Immigration Service performed disgracefully!"

Ironically, the best-known politician from Massachusetts, Senator Ted Kennedy—who made a guest appearance at St. James along with the Mayor, state politicians, and other congressional representatives including Senator Kerry—was in 1966 a key senator in developing and helping to pass the current immigration laws. The hypocrisy was truly unfortunate, and sad.

Kerry referred to the raid as "The Bianco disgrace."

Of course, this all made for great six o'clock news broadcasts and newspaper stories. But what message were they sending to the public concerning the rule of law in America—a law originally spearheaded by John F. Kennedy in 1966?

It was clear to me that the media and the politicians were all working from the same script: appeal to public sympathies and demonize the U.S. Government Agents.

I asked myself, *Who is feeding the beast?*

The answer to that question turned out to be: MIRAC. A Carnegie Corporation Case Study, entitled "Reframing the Immigration Debate, How the Massachusetts Immigration and Refugee Advocacy Coalition (MIRAC) Retooled its Communication Strategy," is an astonishing document.

The fifteen-page undated document proved to be MIRAC's roadmap for how they successfully orchestrated and controlled the MBI story by directing and controlling the media and the politicians who never saw a camera they didn't like.

The document stated that, "MIRAC's goal was to steer the story in a direction sympathetic to the arrested workers and their families."

Within hours of the operation, MIRAC called reporters and "Community leaders were identified, given talking points, and issued press advisory, immediately reframing the language of the debate from 'illegal workers' to 'parents with children.'"

They saw that the press wanted more and realized, "We have to give them a story!" So, in the first twelve days following the operation, MIRAC proudly coordinated eleven press conferences and four large rallies. MIRAC framed a March 7th press conference with a headline: "March 6: The Day That Destroyed the Immigrant Family."

A decision was made not to talk policy so MIRAC asked themselves, "Well, what does move opinion and what does resonate? Children and mothers, that's what!"

The message was, "Children are being hurt, traumatized, and separated from their parents. This resonates with the American public." MIRAC continued by stating, "When confronted with the images of crying babies, children and mothers, almost everyone has a strong, direct, and sympathetic emotional response...it is important to find and maintain this resonance to affect the public consciousness."

MIRAC's stated goal was, "to keep the coverage on the crisis strong and to give the elected officials an opportunity to enjoy positive media coverage while advocating for immigrant families."

Well, there was only one problem with that statement—those immigrant families were here illegally!

MIRAC was always searching for the next big story to give the media. In fact, the document stated that "the media came to see MIRAC as a credible source for continuing stories on developments and events."

On Saturday, March 10th, after seeing a MIRAC op-ed in The Boston Globe, I called Special Agent in Charge Bruce Foucart and practically begged him to get out in front of the media onslaught.

"Otherwise," I explained, "we will lose the case in the public arena and kill the morale of the troops!"

He sympathized but said, "Headquarters won't let me!"

The SAC did do one-off interviews weeks after the raid but it was too little too late. Then, a Federal Judge issued a gag order directed at him, preventing any additional interviews on the case.

Malcolm X once said, "The media's the most powerful entity on earth. They have the power to make the innocent guilty and to make the guilty innocent. That's power. Because they control the minds of the masses."

The media is often referred to as the fourth branch of government and responsible for reporting facts relating to the other three branches (executive, legislative, and judicial) to keep the citizens informed. In this case, the media clearly manipulated the public and colluded with MIRAC in order to advance each other's agendas.

The media's philosophy seemed to be, "Don't let the facts get in a way of a good salacious story that equals higher revenues for a dying print media!"

At the end of the day, the real victims of the MBI/MIRAC media debacle were the American taxpayers, American workers, American soldiers, and the illegal aliens who were mistreated.

Of course, the other victims were the agents of the DHS, myself included. We took an oath to enforce the laws of the United States formulated by elected officials and approved by our judiciary, and that was exactly what we did in the Wicked Good Raid.

✔ Passing Around the Wicked Blame

The politicians piled on and called for congressional hearings and a "thorough" DHS investigation of the case because it was "poorly planned and executed" and caused a "humanitarian crisis."

Yet, the Governor's Public Safety head (who oversaw the Massachusetts State Police and reports directly to the Governor) was thoroughly briefed every step of the way by the SAC and myself.

The New Bedford Police Chief had also been thoroughly briefed months before and supported the investigation. He had asked the SAC and I if we could do him a favor and brief the Mayor on the operation so the Mayor wouldn't be blindsided, and in return reprimand the Police Chief.

The SAC and I had agreed and, forty-eight hours prior to the operation, on Sunday, March 4th, 2007 at approximately 2:00 p.m., we travelled to meet the Mayor at his residence with the Chief of Police. We all sat down at the Mayor's dining room table, and the SAC and I identified ourselves as Special Agents with Homeland Security Investigations.

We informed the Mayor that in the next few days, we were going to execute several criminal arrests and search warrants relating to a company in the City of New Bedford and that this company was knowingly hiring hundreds of illegal aliens. We told the Mayor about the horrendous working conditions and informed him that hundreds of agents would be involved in this operation.

The SAC explained to the Mayor that this was an ongoing Grand Jury (secret) investigation and that Federal Rule 6 (e) prohibited us from divulging specific target information, unless approved by the court. We demanded that our briefing be kept confidential as to not tip off the target in any way.

We went on to tell the Mayor that all illegal aliens would be administratively arrested and processed, and that all sole caregivers and pregnant women would be released. We stated that we were working closely with Social Services, as well.

The Mayor was also told that the Massachusetts Congressional Delegation in Washington, D.C. would be notified as well on the day of the operation, and we let him know that the Public Safety Secretary for the Massachusetts Governor had been briefed too.

We had briefed the Mayor over the course of about an hourlong conversation. As we stepped outside and were walking down his walkway toward our vehicle, the Mayor stopped us and softly said to the SAC and me, "This conversation never happened."

I laughed, thinking he was joking.

He said, "No, I'm serious!"

I thought to myself, *How ridiculous for a former local prosecutor, a Mayor, an officer of the court, to make such a stupid statement to two Federal Agents! What would Dad think of that?*

During the course of executing the search warrant simultaneously with the Wicked Good Raid, a fellow agent had asked me to come into Insolia's office and take a look at his appointment calendar. Right there in black and white was an appointment with the Mayor.

The Mayor's words to me as I was leaving his house echoed in my head. It seemed that he knew perfectly well what was going on at MBI and had adopted an attitude of willful blindness.

Once again, I asked myself what had happened to my city. I wondered how these politicians had allowed criminal activity to go on for years, at the cost of national security and employment opportunities for legal citizens.

In the days, months and years following the operation, the Mayor and the Governor tried their best to dance with the media concerning their knowledge of the operation. I was actually embarrassed for them, as I remembered my father always saying, "Tell the truth! People will respect you more for it."

As recently as the ten-year anniversary of the raid, the now former Mayor continued to massage the truth in an online video interview for South Coast Today, previously known as The New Bedford Standard Times. In that interview, after fumbling his words, the former Mayor claimed he had been told that the raid was simply a labor issue. I considered his statements to be revisionist history.

About a month after the raid, I was interviewed in the office of the Special Agent in Charge by several congressional staffers. They regurgitated the same New York Times, Boston Globe and Washington Post disinformation provided by MIRAC. Their presence in the office had a chilling effect and many agents had no desire to arrest anyone now.

I realized that these congressional staffers had been reading the news accounts and had already formulated the opinion that the operation was poorly planned, and children harmed as a result. It was clear that, just like the others, they didn't care to understand the national security implications. I felt that they wanted me to apologize for protecting our national security and for doing a job our government had hired me to do.

Within a year of the Wicked Good Raid, hearings were held at the congressional and state level. Once again, these were focused on the emotions and perceptions of the American public in the aftermath of the raid. Not a word was said concerning the national security implications or the American jobs lost to illegal aliens.

I was never reprimanded or disciplined for any perceived wrongdoing or impropriety related to the raid, nor were any of my fellow agents. From my perspective, the entire, long drawn out, torturous wicked aftermath—which dragged on for years!—was nothing more than political grandstanding designed to get the faces of democratic political officials on the six o'clock news. It was all a big show.

It was time to break out The Serenity Prayer yet again.

During this time, I also began to practice mixed martial arts. Besides learning self-defense, the mixed martial arts practice truly helped me understand that conflict begins and ends from within. Even in actual fights, the greatest obstacle we face is our own fear, our own breath, or our own tension.

A martial artist starts with this simple fact in mind: The battles will be won when we're willing to face ourselves. I discovered throughout my mixed martial arts training that there were many uncomfortable moments—just like there are uncomfortable days on the journey of life. But in life and in my training, the key is to identify my limitations and work through them.

✔ Rethinking Our Immigration Policies

B ack in 1996, a law was signed by then President Clinton called The Illegal Immigration Reform and Immigrant Responsibility Act. It called for the U.S. Government to capture biometrics for inbound and outbound travel of U.S. visitors. To date, the U.S. Government still has not implemented a biometric exit tracking system, only an entry tracking system. If an exit-tracking system had been in place prior to 9-11, it would have identified five of the nineteen hijackers who had overstayed their visas.

Under President Obama, DHS's National Security Entry-Exit Registration System (NSEERS) would have improved our entry tracking system *and* implemented an exit tracking system. It would have required foreign visitors from high risk countries (Iran, Iraq, Syria, Sudan, and Libya, among others) to provide biometrics and be subjected to further scrutiny. Sadly, the program was dropped before it ever got off the ground because it was deemed "too costly."

The U.S. Government's best estimate is that forty to fifty percent of all visitors don't depart when required. The Department of Justice reported that, from 2001 to 2010, thirty-six of four hundred individuals convicted of terror-related offenses were overstays. In 2015, The Department of Homeland Security estimated five-hundred-and-twenty-seven overstays in America.

On December 24th, 2009, two-hundred-and-eighty-nine people aboard a Northwest Airlines flight from Amsterdam, Netherlands to Detroit, Michigan nearly died because of the U.S. Government's failure to implement an exit-tracking system for visitors who have been issued visas by our overseas embassies and consulates.

The State Department, which issues visas in collaboration with DHS, failed to determine that Christmas bombing suspect Umar Farouk Abdul-Mutallab had a U.S. visa until after he nearly set off explosives in his underwear while aboard a U.S.-bound airplane.

This terrorism attempt occurred *after* the would-be terrorist's father walked into the U.S. Embassy in Nigeria and told officials that his son was associating with Islamic terrorists and may have gone to Yemen. Needless to say, this information wasn't a red flag as much as a burning flag. Yet, the State Department's initial check of the suspect based on his father's information failed to disclose that Mutallab had a multiple-entry U.S. visa because Abdul-Mutallab's name was misspelled.

Our land borders are porous and we fail to properly track visitors to the U.S. and confirm their departures. Only by allocating resources and passing laws can we prevent these groups from operating. Our continued failure to do so will result in many, many more deaths.

Most European and Middle Eastern countries require outbound visitors to present themselves to an immigration inspector to capture biometrics. This is done by swiping one's passport into a computer and then receiving an outbound stamp in their passports.

By identifying past visa overstays so they can be denied future entry, a biometric exit system would also serve as a deterrent to future visitors from overstays. While living in the United Arab Emirates for over four years, I learned that they have no overstay issues because of their inbound-and-exit tracking system, their policy to issue fines for each day you overstay your visa, and their policy to blacklist visitors for repeat offenses.

When in the UAE, you are truly a guest in their home. They welcome anyone—but you must obey their laws, regulations, and customs or you will be asked to leave and may not be allowed back. The U.S. could learn from our UAE brothers and sisters.

Our elected officials must make it their number-one priority to keep America safe from terrorism and international criminal groups. In addition, Congress must immediately allocate resources and hold DHS and the State Department responsible for implementing a vigorous inbound-and-outbound computerized tracking system. Our very existence depends on it.

Otherwise, we should just do away with any pretense of having immigration laws, and open the borders. We will then become much like Colombia and Brazil where the wealthy live in gated communities with armed guards and the lower class are victimized by endless street crime.

✔ Cultivating Confidential Informants

Illegal immigrants can sometimes be cultivated to become Confidential Informants, and serve as the eyes and ears for Law Enforcement Officers. For example, I cultivated an illegal alien I arrested in the Wicked Good Raid to be my Confidential Informant. In exchange he would be allowed to stay in the United States and lawfully work.

Over the years, "Jose" proved his loyalty, resulting in an international drug seizure and information that led to arrests of violent gang members.

Every year before Christmas, Marie and I would give Jose over a dozen garbage bags filled with clothes, books and toys for his impoverished family living in his home country.

When I told Jose that I was moving out of the country, he began to cry.

"Brother, you saved my life and helped my family. I will never forget you. I love you." He always called me his brother.

Those three words are not words a supervisor usually hears from a CI. Yet, I could honestly tell him, "I love you too."

Another Confidential Informant I cultivated was a Middle Eastern man named "Joe" who I met through the law enforcement community. Joe had served in his country's military and proved helpful in providing national security intelligence to me.

One day, Joe tried to prove his loyalty to me in a surprising way. He was at lunch with me and another supervisor named "Mike."

I was expressing my desire "to do" a bad guy, and going on about how badly I wanted to get him.

Joe interrupted and said in his broken English, "Eric, don't say his name…" He motioned to his lips and made a gesture of sealing them shut.

"…Here," he continued, "just write his name down on this piece of paper and I will take care of him for you."

Mike was looking at me in disbelief like he wanted to say, "Hey! Wait a minute here! Did I just become part of a conspiracy to kill a drug smuggler?"

"Joe," I said quickly, "in America, the government can't kill people just because we think they are bad. We have strict rules about prosecuting bad guys!"

These stories about Joe and Jose perfectly illustrate how truly grateful illegal alien Confidential Informants can be when they are given a second chance to stay in the best country in the world. Oftentimes they are more grateful to be in America than U.S. citizens.

Confidential Informants (CIs) are the lifeline for many successful investigations and prosecutions. Yet, they can be the downfall of Special Agents, if not carefully monitored by the controlling agent and his/her supervisor.

Remember, with a CI, we're usually dealing with a bad guy who has agreed to flip on his criminal associates. After all, you can't send a swan into the sewer to catch a rat. You need another rat to catch a rat. Any time you're dealing with a rat, you have to stay alert and remember that they can turn on you in a New York minute. Some have done exactly that. I have actually arrested several for not playing by the agreed-upon rules.

The Whitey Bulger case is a classic example of how CIs can jeopardize an agent's career if the agent is not switched on. Whitey Bulger was an informant for the FBI and was feeding the Bureau information on the Italian mafia. At the same time, Bulger was disregarding the policies and procedures CIs are required to follow and was involved in killing people.

His handler (the controlling FBI agent) knew what Bulger was doing—but he was not properly controlling him because he felt that the ends justified the means. In this case, the "ends" meant all the attention the FBI was getting for prosecuting big organized-crime figures. An FBI agent lost his job, went to trial, and was sentenced to decades in jail. Other FBI agents were also prosecuted over the Bulger case.

The Whitey Bulger case is full of lessons. It reminds us that there are rules, policies and procedures in place for a reason. Our system of justice is based on fairness and the rule of law, and we have to operate within the system—until and unless it is changed and a new system is put in place.

One last interesting note about Confidential Informants: Contrary to what we see in the movies and on T.V., CIs do not always end up in the witness protection program. It is not an easy task to get an individual into witness protection.

During my years as an agent, we made our decisions on a case by case basis. If we had information or intelligence that led us to believe that a CI was in some sort of ongoing danger, we would offer protection. Otherwise, we merely protected them during an operation but discontinued protection afterwards.

✔ Assigned to Dubai as a Diplomat

In 2008, months after the Wicked Good Raid, an opportunity for a foreign assignment was available in the Middle East. I called Marie from my Boston office and said, "Hey, do you and the kids want to go to Dubai?"

She immediately said, "I have no clue where it's located but if you want to go...let's do it."

We decided to apply for the assignment, and I was selected as the DHS Attache responsible for Dubai, Oman and Iran.

Months later, Marie and I were sitting in Washington, D.C. in a week-long State Department Security Awareness Training for all diplomats. During that week, some of the topics discussed included terrorism threats, "safe rooms" inside our villas and evacuation plans for leaving the country.

At one point, Marie said, "It's a good thing I didn't know these things a few months ago or I wouldn't have agreed to come!"

Her world is made up of flowers and butterflies. She never watches the news and is probably better off for it. My home was always a safe haven after facing the evils of the world due in large part to Marie's flowers-and-butterflies approach to life.

On September 8th, 2008, Uncle Bob came by to pick up Marie, sixteen-year-old Jacob, fourteen-year-old Tyler, and our dog Spirit, and take us to Boston Logan Airport for our flight across the globe. I knew that many family members and friends thought that Marie and I were crazy for taking the assignment, considering the fact that war was raging in the region and Dubai was only forty natural miles from Iran.

We didn't feel crazy—we felt divinely guided. I believed I had done everything I could domestically, and now it was time to go overseas where I could make a difference, forge new relationships, and explore new cultures with my family by my side. Marie and the kids were also looking forward to our international adventure.

✔ Realizing We're Not in "Kansas" Anymore

We had a stopover in Switzerland, and arrived in Dubai a day after we left the States. As soon as we landed, it became clear that we were on very foreign soil. We were surrounded by Arab men and women dressed in their local attire, and many new faces from around the world.

U.S. officials escorted us to our new home in Dubai. The place had five bedrooms, four bathrooms and maid's quarters. We were surrounded by a twelve-foot wall and gate with a property security guard. Unlike our two-acre Cape Cod colonial with two acres of land, this was a compound.

After getting Jacob, Ty and Spirit settled into bed, Marie and I spent a few moments organizing our safe room. Sometime after midnight, we collapsed into our bed.

At 4:30 a.m., we were suddenly startled awake by the sound of a loud male's voice outside our window. It was the muezzin, summoning all Muslims to prayer. It turned out that a mosque was directly across the street with five large speakers on top of the minaret. The call to prayer lasted nearly four minutes. For Muslims, the five daily prayer times called Salat are among the most important obligations of the Islamic faith.

We would soon discover that on Fridays, the Muslim Holy Day, the actual sermons could be heard over the loudspeakers. And, with many mosques close to each other, sound waves of sermons would be heard throughout the area, lasting up to an hour each.

We were visited on our very first day by a Consulate Official who came to inform us that the U.S. Consulate had been evacuated due to an earthquake off the coast of Iran. The earthquake had caused the building to sway and now structural engineers were inspecting the foundation.

It was hard to believe we had slept through an earthquake but I was grateful for the sleep. We had been truly exhausted when we fell asleep the night before, between the eight-hour time difference, saying our goodbyes back home, and deciding what to pack in our suitcases, what to put in storage in Massachusetts and which household goods needed to be shipped over in a container.

Those first few months were stressful, to say the least. We were living on a compound, had no personal vehicle, were dealing with language barriers, trying to navigate the strict dress code, listening to the call to prayer five times each day, and trying to adjust to the many other Arabic/Muslim norms we needed to understand and observe if we wanted to avoid arrest and keep ourselves from getting kicked out of the country.

To make matters even more interesting, we had arrived during Ramadan, the Muslim Holy Month. This was a time when absolutely no eating, drinking or smoking in public was allowed anywhere, from sunrise to sunset.

Marie, who was typically stronger than nails, had a few tearful moments. Especially when we were out shopping at a grocery store and security asked her to leave because one of her bra straps was exposed.

Once the kids were settled into The American School of Dubai, life in the desert started to feel like home. Within months, the boys had a chance to travel to Africa, for "A Week without Walls" to learn firsthand about its culture and see the poverty and beauty of the land and animals.

One night early into my tour as I drifted off to sleep, I was awoken by a call from the Embassy. Unfortunately, in addition to my usual workload, I was assigned as State Department Duty officer on call that weekend.

Great! I thought. *Like I don't already have enough DHS work to handle!*

The male caller was calling from the U.S. to inform the Consulate that his sister was visiting Dubai and was arrested for kissing her boyfriend in the back of a cab. The caller said that the cab driver was upset by the public display of affection and had driven the couple to a police station where his sister was arrested.

After a few days in jail, a fine was issued—for kissing in public!—and the woman was released with the warning that, if she were ever arrested again for the same offense, she would be facing longer jail time and deportation. She would also be blacklisted and forever barred from entry back into the UAE. The country takes its laws very seriously and all visitors are expected to do the same or suffer the penalty.

✔ Watching My Back

As the lead DHS official in Dubai, my primary responsibilities were to prevent terrorists and international criminals from entering the U.S., and prevent weapons of mass destruction (WMDs), be they nuclear, radiological, chemical or biological, from entering the U.S. via shipping containers.

In addition, much time was focused on preventing Iran from obtaining WMD materials for their various military programs via their front companies established in the UAE. The Gulf States purchase billions of dollars' worth of military equipment from the U.S. in order to be prepared to defend themselves in the event that Iran's nuclear ambitions lead to war against them.

Iran has traded with the UAE for hundreds of years and, in fact, many UAE nationals have Iranian heritage. This makes for an interesting balancing act between the two countries which would otherwise be hostile toward each other. (The religious division between Sunni Gulf States and majority Shia Iran is at the heart of the mistrust between the UAE and Iran. The fear also is that Iran will attempt to influence the region militarily or covertly as seen in Yemen, Syria, Qatar and Oman.)

Between national security work and diplomatic functions, this assignment proved most challenging and rewarding. With several cell phones on me at all times, dinners were routinely interrupted with criminal cases and terrorist threats needing my attention. I would often receive a 3:00 a.m. call from someone in Washington, D.C. who didn't care that we were eight hours ahead of the East Coast. Work was truly twenty-four hours a day, seven days a week.

In addition to my work responsibilities, the U.S. Consulate was located in the World Trade Center in Dubai and was a known top target for terrorists. UAE State Security (their CIA) was keeping a watchful eye and ear on us too.

We were also constantly surveilled by Iranian intelligence. The Iranians worked overtime in Dubai to gather information on us. On at least one occasion, they tried to infiltrate the Consulate by recruiting a non-American staff employee (a locally engaged staff member), who admitted to being interviewed by Iranian Intelligence on several occasions while visiting Iran.

On one particularly sobering day, the President of Iran in a Dubai newspaper article outed a colleague of mine as a CIA Agent. And a year before I arrived in Dubai, former FBI Agent/CIA contractor Robert Levinson travelled to Kish (an Iranian Island off the Dubai coast) for a meeting. He was last seen in a 2010 video wearing an orange jumpsuit. To this day, his whereabouts are unknown.

To ensure that I was able to escape in the event of an attack, a fellow agent who was leaving his post had left me an industrial spindle of rope in my twentieth-floor office. No one really knew whether the rope was long enough to reach the ground, and thankfully I never had occasion to find out.

Due to our proximity to Iran, the U.S. Consulate where my office was located was visited daily by Iranians attempting to obtain a visa. Each day, the line of people would stretch for a block as applicants were screened by security. They were all hoping and praying to receive a visa so they could travel to America to study, seek medical care or visit a dying relative.

I would later see some of these same folks, some overjoyed because they had gotten their visa, but many distraught because they were refused a visa and had to return to an oppressive country.

I found the Iranian people to be kind and loving, much like the Arabs. Unfortunately, their country was ruled by religious leaders who believed they were acting on behalf of their God, Allah. The supreme leader was Head of State and appointed for life, and the country was run very much like a military dictatorship, with extreme suppression of many basic rights and freedoms of expression we take for granted in the States.

The authorities censored all media, prohibited anything that they deemed un-Islamic, and had dominion over even the smallest detail of life. This included things like music and mixed-gender parties. Any perceived threat was eliminated, and anyone who broke the law was subjected to torture and/or cruel punishments like flogging and amputation. Torture and ill treatment of detainees was common and often used to force confessions.

I had an opportunity to meet with one Iranian male who described to me the torture he underwent as a student activist. He was held for months and beaten about his body with a stick. He had me feel his head which was covered in lumps from the beatings.

The Iranian government and military were always on war footing and showing off their latest military hardware in the Arabian/Persian Gulf. They often threatened Israel with war, continued to support the terrorist group Hezbollah with weapons and funds, and had troops in Yemen, Iraq and Syria.

I was assisting in gathering information that proved that the Iranians were utilizing U.S. dual-use and military components to make Improvised Explosive Devices (IEDs) for use against U.S. Forces in Iraq and Afghanistan. The Iranians were and continue to be heavily engaged in the procurement of WMD materials for their various military programs directed at Israel and the United States. (In the late 2000s, a task force in the U.S. successfully took down an Iranian procurement network which funneled U.S. Technology to Iran via Dubai.)

I also travelled to Miami to interview one of the arrested subjects related to the investigation on Iran's acquisition of IEDs. The subject had agreed to enter into a proffer agreement—a written agreement between Federal Prosecutors and individuals under criminal investigation which permit these individuals to give the U.S. Government information about crimes in exchange for some assurance that they will receive leniency during prosecution.

After spending a day speaking with him, I realized that he wasn't to be trusted.

Interestingly, after returning back to Dubai, a newspaper article stated that the President of Iran was requesting a prisoner swap. He wanted the very same U.S. prisoner I had just spoken to in Miami to be returned to Iran. The exchange never happened.

✔ Staying Switched On in Dangerous Times

The U.S. Consulate was often on alert due to terror. At least once a year, a terrorist group was planning or discussing an attack on the Consulate. Occasional bomb threats also kept everyone on edge.

On occasion, I would tell my staff, "Tomorrow is a good day to work from home."

UAE authorities did arrest a group with chemicals, explosives and police uniforms. And in 2010 in Britain and Dubai, authorities intercepted two parcel bombs destined for the United States. The powerful explosives and detonating mechanisms were hidden inside a computer printer's ink cartridge and were set to explode in the United States.

Dubai was also the scene of several international assassinations while I was in the country.

On January 19th, 2010, a Hamas Leader was killed in his Dubai hotel room. This assassination was put on public display by Dubai Police who proudly displayed surveillance video of the alleged twenty-six Israeli agents prior to the attack.

Ten months earlier on March 29th, 2009 a top Chechen Army General was shot and killed presumably by Russian agents. This put Dubai Police and Customs on alert.

Then, on October 24th of that year, I received a call from my sleepless boss at the Embassy to respond to Dubai Airport.

Evidently, the entire Federal Air Marshal Team (FAM) was detained and was being interrogated and searched. An agent of the team failed to follow established protocol and Dubai Customs discovered a loaded magazine clip for the agent's weapon in his backpack.

This was not good. I knew that if the entire team was arrested, getting them out of jail could take days, weeks or even months. I was aware of at least one case where an American sat in jail for months before ever being charged with a crime.

I was switched on and knew I had to act fast. As I drove, I called senior Customs and Dubai Police Officials and told them how very upset I was over their actions. I also stated that I had spoken to the U.S. Ambassador who was notifying the UAE Minister of State.

This was a total bluff, and I was praying I could pull it off.

I arrived dressed in a business suit. I knew I had to be on my A game if I had a prayer of getting these guys released. So, I immediately took on a persona that was part Robert De Niro and part polished diplomat, and tried to appear as intimidating and important as possible.

As I was escorted into an interrogation office, I quickly glanced over at a bench. There sat a bunch of unhappy looking men who I presumed to be the FAM team. As soon as they realized who I was (after overhearing telephone conversations in which it was stated that a representative from the Consulate was on the way), they appeared noticeably happier.

I didn't acknowledge them at first. Instead I made a beeline for two UAE officials sitting behind a desk—a Dubai Customs Officer and a Dubai Police Officer.

They stood almost in a salute manner to welcome me.

I said, "Assalamualaikum," meaning, "Peace be upon you."

This is a common greeting and it was well received.

I told them I was the Head of U.S. Homeland Security in Dubai and with a stern-but-careful-not-to-be-disrespectful tone of voice, I told them how upset I was that these U.S. officials travelling on "official" passports were detained and searched. I added that the American Ambassador was furious and calling his counterparts with the UAE government.

I demanded that these officials be released immediately. I was careful to use the word officials rather than agents. In the region, "agent" meant CIA and CIA meant spy, and anyone deemed to be a spy was in danger of being prosecuted and/or executed.

They apologized for the "misunderstanding."

I graciously accepted. Then I turned to the FAM Team Leader and said, "We've got everyone...let's go now." And we hustled out.

✔ Preparing to Vacation at Home

After a year in the country, with school now out, the whole family was excited to head back to Cape Cod. We couldn't wait to see family and escape the extreme desert heat which routinely got up to one-hundred-and-ten degrees.

As we stood in line, I made eye contact with the United Airlines station manager who was noticeably nervous. At the same time my phone rang. It was one of my agents. I wasn't going to answer but something told me that this call was related to the, "Oh, shit!" look in the eyes of the United Airlines official.

My agent asked, "Eric, are you travelling tonight on United?"

I took a deep breath and said yes.

"Well, there are several suspected terrorists on board!"

I thought, *NO! I just want to go home!*

I was more than ready to get away from all the threats in the UAE, and the calls for assistance from the domestic offices concerning any of the fifty cases we had ongoing.

After much discussion with my agent and confirmation that Air Marshals were on board, I felt comfortable. I believed that these suspects would be watched carefully. I also knew that Arabic surnames were sometimes confused in the government database, resulting in plenty of cases of mistaken identity.

I decided to go ahead and fly.

When Marie asked me what was happening, I figured she and the boys would have a more peaceful flight if they didn't know what was going on until we landed. They had a nice relaxing flight but, suffice it to say, I didn't get any sleep during our fourteen-hour flight.

As we landed, Customs & Border Protection personnel immediately detained the suspects for questioning. What a way to start my family vacation!

In August of 2009, following our several-week vacation, we returned to Dubai so I could resume my assignment. We landed in one-hundred-fifteen-degree heat with ninety percent humidity. It was brutal. Most people didn't venture out until after dark if they didn't need to.

The people of the Gulf are friendly and hospitality is embedded within their culture. I didn't go to one meeting without being offered coffee, tea, water and dates. To say no was an insult.

I was invited to meet with Sheikh Talib, the brother of the ruler of RAK, a neighboring emirate within the UAE. The Sheikh was in charge of RAK's police force. During the course of the day, he welcomed me for lunch in one of his multimillion-dollar villas. After removing our shoes and taking a seat on the floor, an all-male group of us, including his staff, sat down to share and enjoy a utensil-free feast. (No women were permitted to partake in this feast.) It was a humbling experience.

On another occasion during this period of time, Marie and I were asked to represent the Consular General at a concert by Mercedes Ellington. She is the granddaughter of famous big-band jazz master, Duke Ellington. We had access to a V.I.P. room for drinks and hors d'oeuvres, and our seats were in the front row next to the owner of the theater.

As the music played, all I could think about was my dad. He loved Duke Ellington and all of his music, especially *Satin Doll* and *Take the A Train*. The music that night was pure and wonderful and it united people from around the world. It was a joyful night for Christians and Muslims alike.

Then, of course, the inevitable happened. My phone rang.

It was my boss calling from the Embassy in Abu Dhabi—the guy who never slept.

I politely excused myself from my seat and took the call while thinking, *I really want to meet Mercedes Ellington after the show!*

Sadly, that didn't happen. I'm sure the promoter wasn't thrilled that we left on the last note.

It couldn't be helped. We had received intelligence that terrorists were going to smuggle plastic explosives in prosthetic limbs onto U.S.-bound planes. I spent the next three hours on the phone, waking up my UAE counterparts and answering D.C. emails.

I didn't get to bed until 3:00 a.m. Just another day, and night, as a U.S. Diplomat.

✔ Facing Peril in Kabul

In December of 2009, while still functioning as the UAE Attache in Dubai, I volunteered to lead a group of agents into Afghanistan to train the local officials in how to prevent dirty money from being utilized in their economy. Within a few years, tens of billions of dollars of cash had been smuggled into Dubai by corrupt Afghan officials and various organized-crime groups involved in drug smuggling and weapons.

At the time, there were several articles in the press which were critical of the Afghan and UAE failure to stem the flow of "dirty money." The articles stated that the Obama Administration needed to respond.

Afghanistan was leading the world in opium production. Opium sales, along with sales of cannabis (another drug of which Afghanistan is a leading cultivator) produced billions of dollars in cash which then had to be laundered to appear legitimate.

The expanding cultivation and smuggling of drugs put the entire U.S. and international investment in the reconstruction of Afghanistan at risk, and jeopardized any achievements we had made related to women's issues, health, education, and the rule of law.

While I was in Afghanistan, I was also asked to provide a block of instruction on corruption. I thought to myself, *I must be crazy! I'll be lecturing officials from the most corrupt government in the world!*

Nevertheless, I and another agent travelled on a local carrier into Afghanistan. We were to meet up with the other four members of the team at the Embassy in Kabul.

As I looked through the low-cost airline's magazine, there was a small reference to the Kabul Serena Hotel. We would lecture and train the Afghan authorities there and sleep at the Embassy for security reasons.

According to the advertisement, "After the suicide bombing that took place, security measures have been implemented at the Kabul Serena Hotel."

I thought, *Welcome to Afghanistan!*

We landed, were given bulletproof vests to wear, and were escorted in an armored vehicle to the Embassy where we were issued weapons. The accommodations certainly did not bear any resemblance to the Shangri-La Hotel.

On the Embassy grounds were numerous barracks-style buildings used for lodging. All six of us agents slept in a single room with just enough space for three bunkbeds. The six of us shared four showers, which were also used by ten other rooms. A member of my team was named Ed. So, I knew I was going to be safe, and that Eddie's spirit would be with me during this difficult assignment.

Most nights, we were required to stay inside due to the threat of rocket attacks. Ed was a character who was often up all night, walking the halls. If anyone on the team felt ill, he had them covered. His bags were filled with so much over-the-counter medication, we had our own personal walking pharmacy.

There were times when I was grateful for Ed's meds. The environmental conditions were harsh, and pollution caused me and many others to get a respiratory infection. As for the food…well, we were lucky if we could eat a meal and not get a stomach virus. Some days, I wasn't so lucky.

Each morning, we would load up in two vehicles, wearing our heavy Kevlar vests and carrying weapons for our twenty-minute journey to the Serena Hotel. Once those Embassy gates opened and we were moving, we were no longer safe and we all knew it. Very few words were spoken during those moments.

As we approached, the Serena appeared like a prison. There were Afghan police and soldiers with automatic weapons outside, on the rooftops and inside. All vehicles entered through a sally port similar to that found in a U.S. prison or jail and was then swept for explosives.

The Afghan officials began to arrive. Everyone awaited the arrival of the U.S. Ambassador, who was on his way to present opening remarks.

I immediately met with the hotel Security Director who showed us the safe room to escape to if needed. It was down two flights of stairs in the kitchen.

One day, while attending the training, I was sick and returned to the Embassy to rest.

Suddenly, Ed came into the room noticeably upset. He mentioned how he was in the front right seat of the lead vehicle as they approached a checkpoint and the driver failed to obey an order. Four heavily armed Afghan soldiers surrounded the vehicle and aimed their weapons at Ed and other members of the team. After a few moments of chaos, cooler heads prevailed and the team was allowed through.

Ed kept saying, "It was a *Jesus, Take the Wheel* moment, Eric!"

The very next morning, we geared up as usual. I was sitting in the front right seat of the lead vehicle and Ed was sitting directly behind me. Once ready, I gave the order to roll.

The Embassy gates opened and Ed began to play on his phone the song *Jesus, Take the Wheel* by Carrie Underwood. We listened to it during the entire journey to the Serena. I asked him to play that song each morning from that day on.

✔ My Last Night in Kabul

My last night in Kabul, I went to bed with my bags packed and myself fully clothed for the 3:00 a.m. wake-up call. I wasn't about to miss my ride to the airport. I would be travelling alone, as my agent would be staying behind for a few extra weeks of further work.

Kabul at that hour of the morning was scary and dark, without streetlights. I saw stray animals, burning trash on the side of the road, and maybe even the unknown suicide attacker in the next vehicle. I just closed my eyes and prayed to make it safely to the airport.

As I arrived back in Dubai before Christmas, I nearly kissed the ground.

Kabul had been a tough assignment for everyone, but our appreciation for life, family and country grew stronger.

Within weeks of returning to Dubai, I was sitting in my office watching Al Jazeera news when I saw images of a fire on T.V. It was a hotel in Kabul...the Serena Hotel! It was being attacked by the Taliban who were killing everyone they could see.

An Al Jazeera reporter was live on air, reporting that he was brought down flights of stairs into the kitchen, into a safe room.

I knew exactly where he was, because I had walked that escape route several times and rehearsed the team's escape plan. Sadly, it was attacked again in March of 2014 by four gunmen who killed nine people, including two children who were shot in the head.

In a New York Times article dated April 29th, 2013, titled "Afghan Leader Confirms Cash Delivery by CIA," then President Hamid Karzai acknowledged that the CIA had been dropping off bags of cash at his office for a decade and said the money was used for "various purposes."

The article mentioned that former and current advisers of the Afghan leader said that the CIA cash deliveries totaled tens of millions of dollars over the past decade and had been used to pay off warlords, lawmakers, and others whose support the Afghan leader depended upon.

Knowing the CIA, I wasn't at all surprised by this. While I and others risked our lives to train Afghan Customs and Police Officials, the CIA was undermining us by giving cash they knew was going to be laundered by corrupt officials and other criminals. The CIA was probably motivated by the agency's interest in bigger fish, and perhaps once again felt that the ends justified the means.

I recalled my lecture on corruption in Afghanistan when a high-level Afghan Customs Official based out of the Kabul Airport raised his hand to ask a question. It wasn't really a question but a statement. With passion in his voice, he lectured me through an interpreter, stating that it wasn't him and his colleagues in the audience to blame for the widespread corruption, but rather senior government officials in Kabul.

I knew he was correct. Ironically, the CIA was perpetuating it.

Once again, it was time for The Serenity Prayer.

I had left my family back in Dubai to go to Kabul to teach anti-money laundering techniques. All the while, I was being double-crossed by the CIA.

I thought to myself, *Look, guys, I was risking my life there to prevent money laundering and you were fueling money laundering. What the f**k!*

✔ Appreciating Home More than Ever

After nearly three years, I was ready to return to the States. In March of 2011, my sleepless boss invited me to the Embassy in Abu Dhabi. During a meeting, he announced to the room that it was a good thing that he and I were going home.

"Apparently," he said, "the locals want us out!"

He explained that we had been doing good work (keeping America safe). Obviously, in the process, we had made some locals uncomfortable, and maybe even some entities within the U.S. Government.

I was glad that my boss saw it that way—as a badge of honor.

During our stay, Jacob and Ty had a few interactions with local men that caused them concern. The boys were questioned regarding their feelings about George Bush and the Gulf War.

They had been trained by me to answer that they were from Canada, and loved hockey, maple syrup, and all things Canadian. From time to time, they went off script and admitted that they were Americans.

"Sorry, Dad!" they explained, "The questions were coming at us fast and furious!"

After a few of those encounters where they were caught off guard and got tripped up, the boys memorized their Canadian cover story.

I witnessed it firsthand when we were out to dinner one evening and the waiter asked where we were from. Without hesitation, Ty said, "Canada."

I was impressed that the boys' alternate identities had become engrained in them.

Then, as we were leaving Dubai for our final time, we were all standing at the Immigration desk. The UAE official had all of our black, U.S. Diplomatic Passports to review and stamp.

Ty was up front, leaning on the Immigration Officer's desk, when the officer asked him, "So, where are you from?"

Again, without any hesitation Ty responded, "Canada!"

I looked him and said, "No, not this guy, Ty! He's got your Diplomatic Passport. You want to go home, smart ass!"

I had to chuckle over this. It was the one time that the boys needed to tell the truth about where they were from, but they were so in character, they stuck with it.

As an American family living in the Middle East, we grew closer together, and came to recognize that *all* people, including Muslims, want the same out of life—peace, love and happiness.

I believe that the U.S. can learn life lessons from our Muslim brothers and sisters concerning hospitality, respect for everyone including elected officials, and respect for the rule of law.

✔ Adjusting to Culture Shock

Returning to the U.S. proved to be challenging for the entire family, especially Jake and Ty. They had lived in the Middle East in a large villa with a maid, and travelled to foreign countries such as Sri Lanka, Oman, South Africa and Tanzania.

Traveling gave the boys a window into the lives of others. They discovered new cultures, learned new languages and grew emotionally and mentally. It offered them an opportunity to compare and contrast their lives with the lives of others and it made them not just better Americans but better global citizens.

The psychological, emotional and cultural aspects of reentry proved challenging. As strange as it sounds, returning home was as stressful as the initial departure. We were all experiencing reverse culture shock.

As we had immersed ourselves into a new culture in the Middle East, we became familiar with new practices. We learned new smells, sounds and the overall feel of the new location that became our home.

We made new friends and took on new identities. Eventually, we adapted and became accustomed to our new way of life.

While we were away from the States, our American friends' lives had evolved in one direction and ours in another. When we returned home, we discovered that our old community hadn't grown but shrunk. Relationships that were once strong were no longer quite the same.

If I had any regrets, it was my failure to better prepare Jake and Ty for the reentry. Fitting in proved difficult, especially as the boys were returning to their sophomore and junior years of high school. This was a time of life when belonging and peer acceptance was critical for them emotionally.

The boys had been torn away from their homes, taken across the globe, and now reintroduced to their lives at home. This left them in a position where their life context was so much broader than their peers. Neither of the boys discussed their foreign experience much at all with their peers so as to not come across as conceited.

✔ Reflecting on My Life as an Agent

After so many years of my family and I making sacrifices for my work, I knew my time as a Special Agent for the U.S. Government was coming to an end.

When I first became a Special Agent, I said to myself, *I'll do twenty-five thrilling years as an agent, fulfill my dreams and my dad's, and call it a day. Then, I'll retire, even though I could continue to climb the career ladder.*

Now, as I prepared to retire, I said to myself, *I've made it this far without firing my weapon, haven't lost any personnel in the line of duty, and have never been shot!*

I've been to the mountaintop. I've travelled the world and met with U.S. and foreign diplomats, U.S. Senators and Congressman, and been a guest of the Secretary General of INTERPOL in Lyon, France. I've dined with Sheikhs in the UAE and I've appeared before Congress.

There was no doubt that the job had changed me. Chasing international arms traffickers, drug smugglers, human traffickers, money launderers and counterfeiters, and planning covert national security investigations all took its toll on me and my family.

I had become more cynical after years of arresting criminals and looking into the eyes of child pornographers and molesters. Their occupations ranged from priests to coaches to Law Enforcement Officers, just to name a few, and they were from across the spectrum in terms of age, gender, color, and economic standing.

I had managed to make these arrests without choking out any criminals due to their hideous actions. What proved to be harder was looking into the eyes of babies and children whose abuse was captured on camera or video and then having to notify their parents.

In 2011, I accepted the last position of my career as the Resident Agent in Charge, Homeland Security Investigations, Providence, Rhode Island. It was a rewarding experience to lead a domestic office with state and local officers dedicated to protecting our security.

During this final farewell position as a Special Agent, I led the state's largest counterfeiting investigation, resulting in the seizure of over one million dollars of counterfeit NBA and NFL sporting apparel. I also oversaw the successful prosecution of more than a dozen child pornographers.

✔ Ending My Career as it Began

One day over lunch, I shared my life philosophy with another agent from my office. I talked to him about what my dad had taught me—that tomorrow is promised to no one and we must live like we are dying.

Days later, my career would end much like it began, with the sudden death of a family member. On January 26th, 2012, the office was about to execute an operation when my cell phone rang. It was my sister Cheryl.

"Eric, it's Andrew!" my sister said, crying. "He died in a car accident!"

"Oh, my God, Cheryl...no!" I said. "When? And where? What happened?"

"About an hour ago in New Bedford...on the way to school."

Andrew was our sister Susan's seventeen-year-old son. Sadly, Susan had also lost a beautiful daughter Jennifer at five years old due to a genetic birth defect.

I immediately told my staff what was happening. I also made eye contact with my colleague with whom I had shared my life philosophy just days earlier. No words were said. We just shook our heads.

I left the office to find Marie and share this sad news with her. We travelled to the local hospital to gather with my family. It was extremely difficult. Language is simply inadequate at the moment of death.

The day that Andrew died, I was in the E.R. with Susan when she looked at me, horribly upset, and said, "I just got over Jennifer! Now, look what I have to deal with...my poor Andrew!"

Andrew had attended Greater New Bedford Regional Voc-Tech High School (my high school) and was a popular athletic boy.

Once again, the services were held at St. James Church, and attended by nearly a thousand people. The outpouring of love for Andrew was incredible and deeply appreciated by our family, and especially Sue and my brother-in-law Bruce.

Everyone shared their grief and special memories, much like with my dad's and Eddie's services. The attendees were mostly high school kids throughout the South Coast of Massachusetts who had played sports with Andrew or knew him through friends or by reputation.

During the funeral mass, Andrew's Head Baseball Coach, Rick Avila (my high school class and football teammate) stood and offered some inspirational, heartfelt words about Andrew. Then Coach Rick asked everyone in attendance to stand and applaud for Andrew.

This took me back to my father's standing ovation thirty-one years earlier. There wasn't a dry eye in the church. Unbeknownst to me, Coach Rick had also attended my father's funeral and recalled the standing ovation given for Dad. He wanted to offer the same for Andrew.

Most of the mourners were crying in disbelief, including my nephews (Andrew's cousins) seventeen-year-old Jordan, fifteen-year-old Justin, and twelve-year-old Jared who were sitting alone in an empty adjoining room, consoling each other.

I went over to comfort them, much like Uncle Bob did for me at my Dad's wake. I tried to find those healing words to share in the fog of death—bad weather I had travelled through on too many occasions.

We all lose sight of the fact that the minute we are born, we begin to die. And, of course, as my father used to tell Eddie and me, the hour of death is unknown.

As I sat with the boys and cried with them, I shared the fact that they and Andrew are genetically bound together.

"Guys," I said, "Andrew is with you right now. He's in your DNA… in your hair, skin and eyes. So, each morning when you look in the mirror, you're looking at not only yourselves but actually Andrew too. He'll always be with you."

Each year, family and friends remember Andrew with a benefit dance, the proceeds of which go to benefit various sporting teams along the south coast of Massachusetts. Andrews's spirit lives on through charity.

Eddie's spirit does too. When my twin died, a scholarship was set up in his name at New Bedford High School. It is still active today and has been awarded to a football player each year since my brother's passing. (Our family funded it through fundraising efforts.) These acts of kindness and generosity demonstrate that dying is proof of life.

Just like his cousin Andrew, Jared was an outstanding baseball player for the Greater New Bedford Regional Voc-Tech High School. His performance propelled the team into school history. In May of 2017, during his senior year, Jared's team won the Division 2 State Championship for the very first time in the school's one-hundred-and-one-year history.

Coach Rick visited Andrew's grave on the morning of the championship game. When they won the game, Coach Rick dedicated the win to Andrew and presented a winning game ball to my sister Sue and her husband Bruce.

After the win, Coach Rick was surrounded by the local media. He pulled out a pin made in honor of Andrew shortly after his death, and told the media that he had kept this pin in his pocket during the entire season as a symbol of life and inspiration.

I knew that Jared, meanwhile, had much more than a pin in *his* pocket the entire season. He had Andrew himself with him.

✔ Retiring as a Special Agent

D ue to the incredible stress that the job puts on a Special Agent's mind, body and spirit, the mandatory retirement age is not sixty-five but rather fifty-seven. So, I could have stayed on for an additional eight years. But, every smart spider knows when it's time to come in out of the rain. And every smart fighter knows when it's time to hang up the gloves and leave the ring while you still have your brain intact.

I knew it was time for me to retire. I had worked the requisite twenty-five years and was now eligible for my pension.

So, on July 1st, 2014, just shy of my forty-ninth birthday, I retired as a U.S. Government Special Agent after more than twenty-five years of service. (Ironically, thirty-three years earlier, on July 1st, 1981, my dad died. I didn't even realize the symmetry of that until much later.)

As I retired, I was pretty much intact mentally and physically. I had managed the best I could to balance family responsibilities with the demands of a Special Agent. Marie, Jacob and Ty taught me how to appreciate life and trust the good in all people.

Now, there would be no more jumping every time the phone rang or sleepless nights contemplating a covert operation. No more making sure I left the house with my badge and credentials, "Bat phone," and weapon(s) on me.

My time "in the arena" had come to an end. I had enjoyed a long and decorated career. My professional accomplishments are a testament to how well my father prepared me for my life's work. I know he is even more proud of how he raised a compassionate and heartfelt son devoted to God, family and country.

In a 1966 Father's Day article in <u>The New Bedford Standard Times</u>, my dad was featured along with all of us kids. Dad was quoted as saying that, "All I hope is that my children will grow up good."

We did, Dad...we all did!

✔ Returning to Dubai for an Encore

After I retired, Marie and I sold our home on Cape Cod and built a home in the Southeast. I thought I was completely retired, home free and ready for some decompression and leisure time. I was wrong.

A former British Official from Dubai offered me a position with an international bank. I would be the Regional Head of Operational Intelligence & Liaison within the Financial Intelligence Group for Middle East and North Africa for HSBC.

Interestingly enough, prior to me retiring, the bank was issued a 1.2 billion-dollar penalty by the U.S. Government for its role in money laundering and Iranian sanction violations. My job was to lead a group of analysts who identified financial and reputational risks, and to prevent terror financing.

This assignment would be different. I would be alone.

Jake was attending a university in Massachusetts, Ty was attending a community college in North Carolina, and my wife and I had reached an impasse in our marriage. It proved to be a painful, lonely time—a time of great uncertainty.

On January 5th, 2015, I was in business class by myself, flying over Europe. I was sipping a glass of wine and trying to keep myself together. I couldn't quite wrap my head around the fact that the future of my marriage was in question, after I had just finished twenty-five years with the U.S. Government and built a beautiful new home.

As I arrived back in Dubai, families of U.S. servicemen were suing HSBC for facilitating the movement of monies to U.S.-sanctioned Iranian banks. These banks were controlled by their military (Iranian Revolutionary Guard)—banks that were responsible for many dozens of IED deaths, including the deaths of U.S. Servicemen.

If you'll recall, just five years earlier, I was in Dubai as a U.S. Diplomat assisting domestic agents in investigating the Iranian network responsible for funneling U.S. goods to Iran for IEDs.

While carrying such a heavy load in terms of my fractured home life, it is not surprising that my year in Dubai turned out to be an emotional rollercoaster ride. Concentrating at work was nearly impossible and my boss knew it. I was living in a five-star hotel with wonderful service, but I returned to my room alone at night.

I would walk for hours around the fountain at the base of the world's tallest building, Burj Khalifa, contemplating my life's direction. This was surely a reminder that money can't buy happiness.

When Marie did visit, I would roll out the red carpet. We saw Sting and Michael Buble perform and travelled to adventurous places like the Maldives and Egypt to celebrate our twenty-fifth wedding anniversary.

Our visit to Egypt was especially memorable. The people were very kind even though they had very little. Most of the girls and boys wanted to take photos with Marie and me while touring the pyramids.

We decided, along with our lovely tour guide, to purchase bags of candy and return hours later to distribute them. This gave us a chance to get to know the locals better. As everyone expressed their gratitude, Marie and I had our diplomat hats on and enjoyed listening and sharing.

Very few Americans visit Egypt these days. So, this was the Egyptians' chance to see that not all Americans think all people from the region are terrorists.

On December 29th, 2015, after spending the holidays together as a family in Massachusetts, Marie and I returned to Dubai together, despite the fact that our marriage was already on shaky ground. (Jacob and Tyler stayed behind in the U.S. They were nineteen and twenty-one by then, and living as roommates in an apartment in the greater Boston area.)

Fireworks were scheduled to go off on New Year's Eve atop the Burj. On the morning of New Year's Eve, Marie wasn't feeling well. So, we discussed staying in that evening and cooking a meal. We planned to watch the fireworks from our window, even though we had passes to a V.I.P. event in the garden.

I left Marie in bed while I went to work for the day. I arrived back at the apartment after work to find her feeling noticeably better. We had a lovely meal and decided to get dressed and make our way to the garden, after all. As we exited the elevator, the hotel was packed with guests.

As we headed to the garden, Marie said, "I forgot my tiara!"

I asked if she wanted me to go back upstairs and get it for her.

She thought for a few seconds and said, "There's too many people inside. It will take a while for you to get an elevator, so never mind, but thanks."

We walked approximately twenty yards and sat at the outside bar to have a New Year's Eve drink prepared by our friendly waiter. We enjoyed our cocktails and took a few photos.

I had my back to the hotel when Marie said, "Is that a fire?"

As I looked, I could see that it was indeed a fire on our apartment side of the hotel, on a lower level balcony. It appeared that it was being fueled by the breeze that night…and something else.

Within seconds, it was obvious to me that this hotel would be a total loss. Unfortunately, I would turn out to be right. I grabbed Marie's hand and headed to the nearest known exit. As you know by now, I was always switched on and aware of my surroundings, and always had an escape plan. This night was no different.

As we made our way downstairs, people began to cry and panic. The man in front of me pulled a fire alarm but the alarm must have malfunctioned because no sound was heard. As we hustled our way outside onto ground level, we were suddenly surrounded by thousands of people.

In the rush to safety, I struck a two-foot tall cement planter box that barreled me over onto the ground. I hit it so hard, my feet left my shoes. I was bruised and sore for days.

Marie helped me up and we kept moving away from the scene. We were captured on CNN/BBC moving through the Dubai Mall. We had nothing except the clothes on our backs, my wallet and a cell phone.

After catching our breath, and notifying Jacob, Ty and family via Facebook that we were alive and changing locations, we decided to walk to a sister hotel.

As our hotel burned, Dubai officials decided that the fireworks display must go on. I was surprised but not shocked. The Arabs are a strong, proud people for whom image is important. So, the television viewing audience saw the fireworks go off as planned, and saw the hotel burning in the short distance.

While the fire was raging, some people were making remarks on Facebook that were critical of how the Fire Department and the Dubai Government were handling the fire. Some of these people were arrested for their Facebook criticisms by Dubai Police. In the UAE, visitors have no expectation of privacy and any insults to the country and its rulers result in arrest and deportation.

At 2:00 a.m., Marie and I were bused with hundreds of others to the Atlantis Hotel on the Palm Jumeirah.

I was up all night, reliving our narrow escape and thinking about how blessed and lucky we were to get out in time. I was also worrying over whether the valuables and passports we had left in the safe in our hotel apartment had survived the fire.

As the fire victims gathered in the morning in a conference room to share heroic stories, my marriage fell apart even further. We had just made it through a literal fire but now it was anyone's guess whether our marriage would end up in ashes.

Days later, after waiting in line all day, police and fire officials escorted us to our apartment at the hotel. We had heard all the horror stories concerning the condition of some of the rooms on the twenty-first floor, so we prepared ourselves for the worse. With hard hats on and the smell of smoke all around us, we made our way up in the single operating elevator.

As we came out onto the twenty-first floor, we looked to the left toward our room, number 2103. The door to room 2105 was gone and nothing, I mean nothing, in the apartment was left but the glass table which had melted down to the floor.

Our hearts sank. We couldn't imagine that our room had fared much better in the fire.

Police and fire officials entered our apartment first and we followed. The firemen turned and yelled to us, "It's a miracle!" The living room was intact, and the dining room was as we left it on New Year's Eve, with plates and wine glasses still on the table.

As we entered the bedroom, though, it wasn't good. The room was pretty much gone, and we lost most of our clothes. It was time to dust off and wash the clothes we could salvage, and throw out the rest.

Thankfully, our valuables and passports in the safe were fine.

We had to make several difficult trips to our room. Each time, it took all day waiting in line, and undergoing a security and checkout procedure, to inventorying our belongings.

Weeks later, Marie travelled to India while I stayed behind in Dubai to finish work.

During this time, I had a taxi driver from Pakistan whose name was Abass. He was twenty-six years old and had been driving a taxi in Dubai for several years. For the entire year previous, he had driven seven days a week, twelve hours a day, without a day off. His pay was less than our minimum wage.

One morning, Abass picked me up from another hotel where I was now living. He was neatly dressed and respectful. Although his English wasn't good and my Urdu (the Pakistani language) was non-existent, I felt a genuine human bond.

Abass became not only my driver but a friend and a brother. I always rode in the front seat with him. Each day when he picked me up, if it wasn't already queued up on his phone, I would simply say, "Hit it!"

Then we would listen to Les Brown's *The Journey of Purpose*, an inspirational video Marie had shared with me before leaving for India. It posed the question, "Do you know why you're here?"

Abass would do his very best to understand the words, and ask me to interpret what he didn't understand. It was food for our souls, and we desperately needed it.

One day I invited him to join me the following day at the hotel for lunch, poolside.

He seemed shocked but the next day he showed up, smiling from ear to ear and wearing the sports jacket I had given him. He wanted so badly for me to sponsor him to come to America to live and work.

I explained that his chances of getting a U.S. visa were slim to none.

During lunch, he said that if he couldn't come to America with me, he would work for me for minimum wage in Dubai, if only I would stay.

I tried my best to explain that I needed to return to the U.S. to work on my marriage and try to rebuild my family.

We spent hours talking about our families and our lives. He showed me some gruesome photos on his phone. A local Pakistani terror group had killed and dismembered a group of men near his village and stacked their body parts on top of each other like a puzzle.

On June 8th, 2016, at 6:00 a.m., Marie and I left Dubai for a second time.

As we said goodbye, Abass was crying.

Before leaving, Marie and I had paid for an English course so he could find another job. He is currently working for Starbucks and still dreams of coming to the United States like so many people from the Middle East Region.

Life's journey is a mystery, full of good and evil. The journey teaches us that forgiveness and reconciliation are essential to our inner peace and happiness.

✔ Taking the Bad with the Good

People tend to envision Special Agents as superhero types who are out there fighting crime and evil, and there is no question that a Special Agent's life is in many respects larger than life. My years as a Special Agent were rich, memorable, satisfying and filled with all kinds of unforgettable experiences—good, bad and in between.

What people don't realize is that it can be a lonely life. During my career, I found it hard to make and maintain personal friendships. Most of the people I encountered in my daily work were criminals and everyone else, unfortunately, was suspect.

I was never comfortable completely trusting anyone. I would meet a potential friend and ask myself, *Is this person genuine and sincere, or could they be a friend of a target? Or, an agent of a foreign government?*

On the flipside of the coin was the equally lonely reality that very few people wanted to be friends with a Special Agent. Many people do what they consider minor law-bending, from cheating on their taxes to smoking weed, so most would shy away from cultivating a friendship with me.

Then there was the reality that all the domestic and international moves that went with the job made it hard to nurture relationships of any kind. This was as true for my wife and children as it was for me.

Sometimes when a new assignment required us to move, we had to pull the kids out of school. As my boys said goodbye to their friends, I often witnessed tears, and it broke my heart. At the same time, I knew that change would provide professional growth for me, and new experiences and friendships for our entire family.

The job itself wasn't always glamorous, either. We were often operating with insufficient budgets and minimal staff. It wasn't unusual for us to be short-handed as we rolled out on surveillance or an arrest. At times like these, I learned to make chicken salad out of chicken shit, so to speak. (That culinary training coming in handy again!)

In every profession and in every aspect of life, we are called upon to take the bad with the good. Those who learn that lesson and make peace with it tend to live much more fulfilling and satisfying lives than those who expect every day to be rainbows and unicorns.

✔ Preserving LEOs' Mental and Emotional Health

Over the course of my twenty-five-plus-year career as a Special Agent, I lost several friends and colleagues to suicide.

According to the Badge of Life, a nonprofit organization with the mission of lessening the impact of both stress and trauma upon police officers and retirees and preventing police suicide, one-hundred-and-eight officers took their lives in 2016. Furthermore, that same year, according to the National Law Enforcement Memorial Fund, one-hundred-and-thirty-five officers lost their lives in the performance of their duty, and twenty-one were ambushed, for a total of two-hundred-and-forty-three deaths. The numbers for 2017 in both categories were similar.

These numbers are staggering—but not surprising when you consider the reality of a LEO's work life. LEOs are in constant fight-or-flight mode, resulting in higher levels of stress. This extreme stress causes physical ailments such as headaches, stomach ulcers and heart issues. What can't be seen and is often undetected is the psychological injury many LEOs suffer in the form of Post-Traumatic Stress Disorder (PTSD) and depression each day in America.

PTSD, this silent killer of LEOs, is responsible for one-hundred-and-twenty-five to one-hundred-and-fifty deaths in the form of suicide each year. Notice I am not using the term "self-inflicted deaths." To do so would represent a naive understanding of the law enforcement culture and heroic actions performed each day.

Much more needs to be done to call attention to this taboo silent killer and to encourage the public, and LEOs' loved ones, to understand that these deaths are in fact job-related injuries to the mind and soul.

PTSD is one cause of suicides among LEOs. Suicides can also be triggered by stressful and/or traumatic events in a LEOs personal or professional life that propel them on a path of self-destruction, or into a dark place.

When I was a Special Agent involved in an operation, I would be consumed by it. I lived my work, day in and day out. I put my head down and focused on the task at hand. My mindset was that I had to do whatever needed to be done, while trying to stay focused on SEE as much as possible.

So, I didn't recognize it immediately when I was suffering from PTSD. And I didn't understand why I, of all people, would be having fleeting thoughts of suicide.

Shortly after I retired and moved into the house my wife and I built, marital challenges began to take their toll on me. I felt all alone in the world and in a dark place. Depression and fleeting suicidal thoughts suddenly crept into my mind, and sleepless nights added to the mental fog.

I had a decorated career and a great family and yet I felt like a total failure. I began apologizing to my family members for perceived mistakes and found myself walking alone for hours on end. I am not someone who would ever seriously entertain taking my life, so I was surprised to have even the most fleeting thoughts of suicide. It was a reminder to stay switched on.

Faith proved pivotal in restoring my positive disposition, as did my family and friends. They helped awaken me and reminded me of my simple but effective mantra of Sleep, Eat & Exercise (SEE). And, I believe that the love of my family members who have already crossed over (especially my father, my twin brother, my mom, and Uncle Pete) also helped me feel like myself again.

It is critical that Law Enforcement Departments offer mandatory, truly holistic wellness training to *all* staff and their families. The families may need help themselves. They are certainly in the best position to recognize psychological injuries in their loved ones and seek help for them. These wellness programs need proper funding. A stress management program without proper funding is nothing more than a paper tiger.

In addition, departments need to encourage a *culture* that promotes a holistic rigorous mental-health program, not just a check-the-boxes program. Professional and peer counseling groups need to be offered to all officers and family members, and become mandatory for LEOs involved in traumatic events.

We as a society also need to be more understanding of our LEOs. They routinely come face to face with evil and death and are asked to perform superhero (superhuman) tasks. They do so the only way they can—as frail, imperfect humans. It can cause extreme stress, depression, and suicidal ideology when LEOs are subjected to scrutiny over their split-second, life-and-death actions and judged by not only their peers, but the law and society as a whole.

I say, the next time a politician criticizes Law Enforcement Officers, or wants to play Monday morning quarterback, let's remind them of these statistics and the spouseless partners and parentless children who will never have a dad walk them down that aisle or be present for a graduation ceremony.

I dare these critics to wear the badge of courage for just one day or night. Then, let's hear what they have to say.

Theodore Roosevelt's "The Man in the Arena" speech from 1910 is a powerful statement to live by: "It is not the critic who counts; not the man who points out how the strong man stumbles, or where the doer of deeds could have done them better. The credit belongs to the man who is actually in the arena, whose face is marred by dust and sweat and blood; who strives valiantly; who errs, who comes short again and again, because there is no effort without error and shortcoming; but who does actually strive to do the deeds; who knows great enthusiasms, the great devotions; who spends himself in a worthy cause; who at the best knows in the end the triumph of high achievement, and who at the worst, if he fails, at least fails while daring greatly, so that his place shall never be with those cold and timid souls who neither know victory nor defeat."

Our LEOs and their families need not suffer in silence anymore. They, and the greater community, will all be better served by LEOs who are not just physically strong, but mentally switched on.

We must all recognize that every LEO life lost to suicide is a result of an on-the-job injury, and work tirelessly for the time when there is not a single tragic suicide by a LEO.

✔ Examining My (Broken) Heart

Just short of my fifty-second birthday, I decided to visit Mass General Hospital for a routine checkup for my heart. Since heart disease took many of my beloved family members early in life, I am vigilant about having my checkups.

When I went to see the doctor, I wasn't too concerned because I religiously follow SEE and I'm in good shape—or, so I thought. But a heart test proved devastating. Although my total cholesterol and LDL and HDL levels were good, my family's demon heart history had finally caught up to me.

I heard those dreaded two words: heart disease. My left main artery had atherosclerosis. As if that wasn't bad enough, I was prescribed a medication that I now have to take for the rest of my life. For someone who had been free of drugs and medication my entire life, this proved to be a difficult adjustment.

The hour drive south alone was emotional. I had to tell my family that the heart of this Special Agent was wounded—but I wasn't going down without a fight. With medication and SEE, I was more determined than ever to beat the odds and "live life like I was dying," just like Eddie and my dad.

✔ Being Switched On for Life

In September of 2017, I began a new career as an Adjunct Professor at the Massachusetts Maritime Academy on Cape Cod, teaching a course on the Prevention of Transnational Crime.

One day the scheduled lecture was on drug smuggling, but God spoke to me and I decided to change the lecture for the day.

"This particular class," I told the cadets, "will be the most important lecture, not of the year, but of your entire lives! And there's no makeup exam if you get this wrong."

I then proceeded to teach them the foundational principle of life that my father had passed down to me and Eddie when we were so young: SEE.

"Sleeping at least eight hours a night, eating right, and exercising daily if possible, and if not, then at least three times a week, is the key to being prepared for life."

I also taught them about the importance of being switched on.

"First," I explained, "we must remember that most predators operate like lions in the bush, or leopards in trees. They are hunters— and they hide, waiting for prey. Predators prefer it when it is dark outside, so be especially alert. The dark provides endless hiding places. Unless they are mentally deranged, predators don't want to get caught. Like the lion, they select the weak or soft targets to attack. So, you must present yourself as a hard target, not a soft one, so the lion passes you over and keeps searching for a soft target."

When the class asked how to do that, I explained that our mere presence conveys a lot. Do we walk with purpose? Are all our senses switched on? Are we tuned into our environment or tuned into our phones, our music, or something else that distracts us and steals our attention?

"Being switched on begins with your mind," I continued, describing how the mind is critical to surviving attacks. "It is the most important muscle in your body when it comes to being switched on. In times of fear, your fight-or-flight mechanism will get triggered. Your body could freeze and become paralyzed with fear. But, if you've trained your mind in advance, that mental training will kick in and catch you like a safety net."

I taught the cadets that their senses—sight, smell, hearing—must also be utilized as tools to identify potential threats, avoid or escape those perceived threats, and identify potential safe havens. I explained that if we fail to identify and avoid potential threats, the odds are greater that we will be attacked and the odds of survival diminished.

I also talked to the class about the reality that, even if we identify a potential threat and attempt to avoid or escape it, there may be times in life when we have no choice but to stand and fight.

"I say stand because one must avoid the ground at all costs. Having a bad guy mount you, throwing punches to the head (your computer) could be deadly. So, why do I call your head your computer system?" I continued. "Because your head is like your safety radar, your threat protector. If being switched on becomes second nature to you, your mental computer will forever be scanning the environment and seeking to identify potential threats and safe havens for escape. And, your threat detector will beep, so to speak, and alert you to danger."

I taught the class this truth: that God has given us instincts and the gifts of our senses and intuition. The hair stands up on the back of our necks for a reason. That is God, somebody upstairs, telling us, "Beware! Something here is not right." If we train ourselves to identify a potential threat sooner rather than later, we will have time to get away.

I told the class what to do if they see a potential bad guy while walking down the street. I told them to make brief eye contact and let them know, "I see you. You see me. Don't mess with me!"

Surprising the class, I told them that I was not an advocate of civilians owning weapons. "Due to adrenaline surges caused by danger and fear, you will not be able to think straight when you need to use that weapon that's been sitting at the top of your closet, gathering dust.

And worse, owning a weapon will give you a false sense of security and maybe even keep you from feeling like you need to be switched on."

I explained that to be protected, you don't need a weapon. "I've already talked to you about training the most important muscle in your body—your brain—so your senses are switched on. You could and should also use your voice as a weapon. It distracts a bad guy from his plan and interrupts its execution. It gives you time to escape and attract witnesses and help."

I also taught the class to listen to a potential bad guy's speech, and to look at their eyes, and check to see if they are concealing their hands. There is a reason that police always tell a person of interest to remove their hands from their pockets. Hidden hands could be concealing a weapon.

"When you're looking at someone from head to toe," I said, "from their skin, to their body, to their clothing, to their demeanor, there is information there to be gained—if you're switched on. For example, if someone walks into a store and it is summertime and they're wearing a down jacket, ask yourself, *Why the hell does he have a jacket on? Is he hiding a gun? Or shoplifting?*"

I taught my cadets to be alert to certain danger signals and to ask themselves these questions: Are this guy's eyes roaming around, looking for witnesses for the crime he's about to commit? Is he standing with his chest out, posturing like a lion? Is he sweating? Is his voice quavering?

"...And, beware of the man on the street who seems to be approaching you with a benign request," I continued. "His words may be saying one thing, but his body and his eyes may be telling you he's planning to attack you. The eyes of a bad guy never lie..."

I reminded the class that, in times of crisis, we can't think straight. So, we must plan in advance. "We must look at our surroundings and plan an escape strategy, just in case. And it's wise to identify both a primary and a secondary exit. When you go to a concert or a theater, for example, always try to sit on the aisle for an easy out."

I explained that being prepared might mean that you walk the steps of the concert hall and count them, so you'll know how many steps are between you and the nearest exit. "...Or, if you're in a dark theater, about to watch a show, physically touch the chairs between you and the aisle, and count them as you go. In the dark, in a crisis, you won't be able to see. If physically doing a walk-through of your escape in advance is impossible, do it mentally."

In closing, I said, "As my dad taught me, and I taught my own kids, tomorrow is promised to no one. So live your life to the fullest. But, be prepared. When you're prepared, you have the ability to say to yourself, *When the shit hits the fan, this is where I'm going and this is what I'm doing—and that is where I am not going and what I'm not doing!* And keep it simple. You don't need a ten-point plan. Just have a simple plan in place…"

In the weeks following this particular lecture to my class, I was asked by several news organizations to comment on terrorist attacks and mass shootings. I shared those news videos with the class, taking the opportunity to remind them of how imperative it is to stay switched on if we are to prevent and survive an attack.

In December, I gave my final exam with an extra credit question: Define SEE.

I am proud to say that all the cadets answered correctly. After the class, one cadet approached me and said, "For as long as I live, I will never forget the importance of SEE and staying switched on."

The responses I received to teaching the SEE and switched on principles helped me remember that there are no accidents in life. I retired when I did for a reason, and it went beyond simply being home to love and support my family.

I hope that all of you will continue to go out into the world and live *your* lives. Don't let terrorists and criminals prevent you from enjoying your blessings. Don't let the bad guys take your freedom away from you. Empower yourself by training your mind and body to be switched on.

✔ Finding Footprints in the Sand

Now that I was a retired Special Agent, I was being given the chance to pass along to others the principles I was taught by my dad—

the same basic principles I practiced firsthand during my career. Dad gave me the basics and experience gave me the rest.

On many mornings these days, I find myself walking on a small beach on campus, reflecting on my life. As I walk alone without Marie, I can almost see another set of footprints in the sand, reminding me that I am never, ever truly alone. My dad and all my loved ones are with me in spirit until we all meet again. It is through love and loss that our hearts take shape and our growth as human beings is guided.

Sometimes I look over at that second set of footprints walking along beside mine and I am reminded of that wonderful poem, *Footprints in the Sand: One night a man had a dream. He dreamed he was walking along the beach with the Lord. Across the sky flashed scenes from his life. For each scene, he noticed two sets of footprints in the sand; one belonged to him and the other to the Lord...* (Author unknown.)

I realize that God wasn't the only one watching out for me all these years. Both my dad and Eddie have been walking beside me as well, and keeping me safe. "Thanks, Chief. Thanks, Dad. Love you!"

Afterword

S o, how have I managed to stay positive and keep my faith after spending so many years fighting crime, criminals and evil? How have I managed to keep from becoming jaded or bitter, like some members of law enforcement who devote their lives to fighting the worst kind of criminals and dealing with the most terrible evil?

When I think of the answer to the question, I see a triangle.

The first side of that triangle is good self-care. I believe my ability to maintain a positive attitude started in my childhood when my father taught me the SEE philosophy. By making sure my siblings and I understood the importance of sleeping well, eating right and exercising daily, he was teaching us to develop a habit of good self-care.

I learned as a kid that whenever things became overwhelming or my emotions threatened to derail me, it was time to do some good self-care. It was time for a break, a time-out. When I became an adult, and started my career as a Special Agent, I was already in the daily habit of good self-care, and I knew how to recognize the signs that it was time for me to step up my self-care.

Sometimes those signs looked like depression, exhaustion or depletion. Whenever things became too much, I took a break, a time-out, just as I had learned to do as a kid. Sometimes a short break was enough and sometimes I needed to completely shut down and check out for a week or two so I could recharge my batteries.

The second side of the triangle is faith and family. The early life lessons about relying on God and family for support, strength and help have stayed with me throughout my lifetime and been my guiding light. Whenever I've been down or feeling less than ideal, I have turned to my family and to God. And sometimes family has included dear family friends who stepped in and became honorary uncles when my father died.

And finally, the third side of the triangle is my belief that good will always prevail over evil. Throughout my career as a Special Agent, I worked many types of cases, including drug smuggling, national security, and human trafficking, just to name a few. Whenever I saw someone who has been victimized or fallen prey to criminals, it was tempting to walk away feeling that evil is so pervasive in the world, and we are so powerless to stop it, I might as well stop trying.

Then I would shake off that feeling and return to the foundational principles that never fail me. I believe we must each continue to focus on the good, move toward it, and do everything within our power and capacity to promote it for our loved ones and those good citizens at home and abroad that we may never meet.

Every time that I arrested a bad guy who had been abusing children; every time I stopped a shipment of drugs from reaching the streets and the hands of our youth; every time I was able to prevent criminals from ruining the lives of good citizens, I had a feeling of satisfaction and fulfillment that my father must have felt when he went to work each day. Every victory confirmed my faith that, at the end of the day, if we continue to fight the good fight, good can prevail over evil.

Even as we're fighting the good fight, and staying positive, we must take great care not to wander off into the land of magical thinking, where we allow ourselves to tune out and pretend that danger and peril do not exist.

We must remain switched on at all times. We need to remain alert and aware while also keeping our hearts and souls wide open. It is a balance that must be struck if we are to live safe, happy, productive lives.

Without that balance, we can slide over to the dark side without even realizing what we're doing, and end up living our lives depressed, paranoid and emotionally closed off. And without that balance, we can also slip into a delusional state of being where we stick our heads in the sand and refuse to deal with reality, setting ourselves up to be preyed upon and victimized.

Seek Balance. Keep faith. Family first. Walk—and live!—with purpose. And remember, remain switched on!

About the Author

Eric J. Caron is a former U.S. Diplomat, U.S. Special Agent, and HSBC Middle East Bank Executive. He is currently a security consultant and an analyst for Channel 7 News in Boston, Massachusetts. He is also an Adjunct Professor at the Massachusetts Maritime Academy on Cape Cod, where he teaches a course on How to Identify and Prevent Transnational Crime, and Cyber Security.

Caron has held senior positions within the Department of Treasury, Department of Homeland Security (DHS) and INTERPOL. Throughout his career, he successfully initiated and managed covert operations that identified and disrupted international WMD proliferation networks, terrorism, terror financing, and transnational crime networks involved in drug smuggling, human trafficking, and intellectual property rights (IPR) violations.

He was the lead DHS official in Dubai, responsible for preventing WMD materials from entering the U.S. and military technology from being acquired by Iran. In addition, he led training in anti-money laundering, counter-proliferation, and border security for UAE and Oman Police and Customs Officials. He also traveled to Afghanistan to lead an anti-money laundering and corruption seminar.

Former Special Agent Caron concluded his career as the Resident Agent in Charge, Homeland Security Investigations, Providence, Rhode Island, where he led the state's largest counterfeiting investigation, resulting in the seizure of over one million dollars of counterfeit NBA and NFL sporting apparel. In addition, he oversaw the successful prosecution of more than a dozen child pornographers.

Caron received the U.S. Attorney General's Award for his "Endeavors in furthering the interests of U.S. National Security." He also was recognized by the Secretary General of INTERPOL. His accomplishments have been reported by media outlets from around the world.

His career highlights include the very first Department of Justice prosecution of several executives who illegally provided a defense service and exported controlled U.S. technology to former Russian military facilities. The imported finished Russian technology was subsequently sold to the U.S. Military. In addition, he arrested a former dean of Moscow University and his Belarus business partner who were attempting to acquire US F-15J radar equipment.

The author is a graduate of Northeastern University, and is a Certified Anti-Money Laundering Specialist (CAMS). He has completed a marathon and a triathlon and is a mixed martial artist.

Eric is one of seven children, and a fraternal twin. His late father was a decorated New Bedford, Massachusetts Police Officer and former Marine.

When he is not lending his knowledge and expertise to the country's continuing fight against crime, evil, and terrorism, Eric is likely to be found spending time with his family, at the gym working out, or walking along the beach.

He believes, as his father taught him, that family, country and God come first. He also believes strongly that, as John Adams once said, "We are a nation of laws, not of men," and no man or institution is above the law.

Life Lessons From The Heart and Mind of a Special Agent

Sleeping eight hours, eating well, and exercising (SEE) are the three most important things you can do daily. My mantra!

§ Faith is like wind. You can't see it, but you feel it. Believing in a greater being gives you hope, and helps see you through those life-shattering phone calls.

§ Education is your ticket to life's party. Without it, you can't get in. It's that simple.

§ Travel gives you a window into other people's lives.

§ Respect is required if you want loving families and communities.

§ Love everyone including your enemies.

§ Forgiveness in large doses is required in life. Do it for yourself! It is the key to freedom.

§ Perseverance is essential. Never, ever give up! To do so is to die emotionally.

§ Friendship is a gift. Find those you enjoy being with, those who feed your soul, and share love.

§ Your life's work is a service to others and should be performed with kindness and compassion.

§ Remain switched on—operating with all your senses, staying alert, and running on all cylinders.

CPSIA information can be obtained
at www.ICGtesting.com
Printed in the USA
FSHW01n1658240418
47410FS